Living in Jesus

meditations for children and adults

Sister Mary J. Steinkamp SNJM

Guardian
B O O K S

Belleville, Ontario, Canada

Living in Jesus

Copyright © 2004, Sister Mary Steinkamp
Illustrations by Sister Helen Moore, SNJM

All Scripture quotations, unless otherwise specified, are taken from the *New King James Version*. Copyright © 1979, 1980, 1982. Thomas Nelson Inc., Publishers.

Library and Archives Canada Cataloguing in Publication

Steinkamp, Mary J. (Mary Julia), 1931-
Living in Jesus : meditations for children and adults / Mary J. Steinkamp.

ISBN 1-55306-743-6

1. Meditations. 2. Catholic children--Prayer-books and devotions--English. 3. Jesus Christ--Meditations. 4. Catholic Church--Prayer-books and devotions--English. I. Title.

BV4870.S73 2004   242   C2004-904037-5

**For more information or
to order additional copies, please contact:**

Sister Mary Steinkamp
2014 NE 19th Avenue
Portland OR 97212

Guardian Books is an imprint of *Essence Publishing,* a Christian book publisher dedicated to furthering the work of Christ through the written word. For more information, contact:

20 Hanna Court, Belleville, Ontario, Canada K8P 5J2
Phone: 1-800-238-6376. Fax: (613) 962-3055.
publishing@essencegroup.com.
Internet: www.essencegroup.com

I dedicate this book to
Bill and Doneva, George and Elaine,
and Darlene and Vince,
who are dear to me;

The terrific staff of the Madeleine School,
especially Maureen, Patt, Bee, James,
and Sister Yolanda,
whose quiet, behind-the-scenes work
helps make the school excellent.

My cousin Cathie,
whose indomitable spirit inspires me.

Pauline, Rosemary, Elaine, Shirley, Shawn,
Harryette, and Peggy,
prayer friends who keep me afloat.

Doris A., whose devotion to Our Lady touches me.

Rhonda, Carole, Lynn, Becky, and Cassie,
whose faith and friendship I value.

Sister Helen M., whose prayerful spirit
and appreciation for the beauty of God in nature
is most uplifting.

Table of Contents

Kindness

Gratitude

Prayer, Faith, Mission, Free Will

Trust and Hope

Eucharist

Mary

Christmas

Resurrection

Pentecost

Acceptance and Belonging

Acknowledgements

The five volumes of *The Poem of the Man-God,* by Maria Valtorta, are each approximately 700 pages long, and filled with details not included within regular translations of the New Testament. We are told in John 20:30, "And truly Jesus did many other signs in the presence of His disciples, which are not written in this book"; also, in John 21:25, "And there are also many other things that Jesus did, which if they were written one by one, I suppose that even the world itself could not contain the books that would be written." For ten years or so, I have used *The Poem of the Man-God* as a resource for my own personal life, and in teaching children to know Jesus. Many of my friends have also read all five volumes.

Maria Valtorta, born in 1897, lived in Italy and never went to the Holy Land. She was not a scholar; in fact, she was sick in bed most of her life. With inspiration from God and the encouragement of a priest, and never from her imagination, she wrote her books. My thanks go to Maria Valtorta, who died in 1961, for completing this series, even though she was so sick at times she could hardly hold her pencil.

These controversial books belong to the private revelations of the Church. They have an imprimatur, but because they are private revelations, Catholics are not obliged to believe them. Nonetheless, they contain a wealth of truth and inspiration, and in my opinion are most helpful for teaching Christian doctrine.

About twenty-nine examples from the five volumes of *The Poem of the Man-God* have been adapted for this meditation book. When I used them in the classroom, they worked well—holding the attention even of eighth-graders! One of the visionaries at Medjugorje asked Our Lady what they should read, and the reported response was to read the Bible and *The Poem of the Man-God*. She also said to watch as little television as possible.

I am grateful to Central Distributors for Valtorta, CEDIVAL INC., P.O. Box 492, Sherbrooke, Quebec, Canada, J1H 5K2, phone 819-346-2233, who very graciously gave me permission to use material from the volumes of *The Poem of the Man-God*.

Thanks as well to Centro Editoriale Valtortiano srl, 03036 Isola del Liri, Italy, reprinted at Isola del Liri, Italy, by Tipografia Editrice M. Pisani sas, for Centro Editoriale Valtortiano srl in 1992, translated from Italian by Nicandro Picozzi, M.A., D.D., revised by Patrick McLaughlin, M.A.

I ask God's special blessing on all these people who made this work possible. I am grateful for their work, and for the many people who have come closer to God through this joint effort. What is especially delightful about *Poem of the Man-God* is that it brings a person insight into the personalities and the very human side of the apostles and others from the New Testament.

—*Sister Mary Steinkamp, SNJM*

Preface

Back in the 1980s, when my seventeen-year-old nephew was dying of a strange virus, his older brother wanted a miracle and we prayed. "You seem to have found God," Peter said to me. "What doctrine do you follow?"

"Oh, Peter, I don't follow a doctrine—I follow Jesus," I told him. Now, I was not disparaging the importance of doctrine—it is important to know the truth and to follow correct teaching. However, without a loving relationship with Jesus, doctrine becomes very empty and sterile. In forty-six years of Christian education, I cannot think of anything as special as sharing faith with children and helping them have a loving relationship with Jesus.

Meditation is one key. That loving relationship with Jesus, to live in Him, is the priceless gift we as educators can inspire. When children become filled with His goodness and lost in His love, their lives will never be the same—and our world will change for the better. As a Holy Name Sister, it is my fervent prayer that this book will help children in that most beautiful and sacred time of their lives.

So, do not allow one child to spoil it for another. At the initial session, have the children go with Jesus to build a secret place: a house, a tree house, a beach place, a ski resort—whatever they prefer. Then, begin each session by having them go to their secret place. When reading the meditations aloud, give them time to think between the lines. It needs to be quiet, prayerful, and reflective. Try to leave all pressure outside.

Parents and catechists can adapt examples to fit their level of interest. Daily periods of five minutes at home are recommended. All meditations bear repeating.

It takes a lifetime to live the good news. These meditations are just a beginning. They will help a child to know Jesus in a new way, and say, with the apostles at Tabor: "Lord, it is good to be here!"

—*Sister Mary Steinkamp, SNJM*

Introduction to
Mini-Meditations for Children

In Him we live and move and have our being,
as also some of your own poets have said....
ACTS 17:28

These meditations are intended for use with children in grades five to eight. While children like to meditate, it is important to keep it brief: for grades four to six, about five or six minutes is right. For grade seven and eight, about seven minutes at the most will be sufficient.

In a classroom, have the children sit around the edge of the room on their prayer mats (rug squares), with their eyes shut, hands open to receive, relaxed, but with backs fairly straight. They may sit by a friend, but leave twelve inches between—no touching. Each child needs a quiet space in which to hear God. Be very strict about cooperation—this is important.

Building Your Meditation House
Building Your Secret Place

The weather is quite warm. You are sitting on your front porch, wishing something interesting would happen on this dull weekend, when Jesus comes and sits down beside you. You are a little startled.

"Come," He says, "let's go build your secret place."

"Okay, but first let me check out with my mom." You call to your mom, "I'm going hiking; I'll be back in two hours."

"All right," she calls from upstairs. You walk with Jesus down the road to a little woods where it's cool and lovely. You feel like you're flying.

"Where do you want your secret place? What kind of house do you want to build?" Jesus asks.

"Wow! You mean I can have anything I want? Absolutely *anything*?"

"Yes, it's all yours, whatever you want—ocean, mountains, cottage, mansion, you name it," Jesus replies. "Today we will build, and then meet there often."

"Let's sit on this log so I can think," you reply. You sit down together and plan your secret place.

"Remember," Jesus says, "this place is so secret no one can find you there. It is perfectly safe. No thief can break in. No one can take it from you. It is yours completely." You are excited. You begin planning. You put windows where you want them. You include trees, flowers, plants, swimming pool, riding horses, everything you want. There are your favorite colors, and the place is the perfect size.

"Can I have my own pet camel if I want?"

"Yes, of course," Jesus reassures you.

"Munch is a good pet. His only bad habit is that he spits when he's mad about anything."

"You can even build a special house for Munch. Put in it anything he likes."

"Licorice, of course!"

Finally, your house and Munch's are ready. They are just right. Jesus sits down with you and says, "I'm glad you have everything where you want it." Then, before He leaves, He promises, "This is only the beginning. Today I have begotten you anew in My love. You are precious in My eyes and I love you."

You listen carefully and carry the words home with you. "What does it mean to be precious in God's eyes?" you ask yourself. "How can I thank Jesus for this special place?"

Your mom asks, "Did you have a good hike?"

"Super, Mom!" You kiss her on the cheek. She is so taken aback, she almost falls into the stew she is stirring.

CHAPTER ONE

Galatia, a Repentant Sinner

Jesus has just finished speaking to a large crowd when He turns around and says, "Who has called on Me for a body and spirit healing?" No one answers. He repeats His question. Matthew replies, "Master, You must be aware that many have sighed for You after hearing Your wonderful words."

"No, a soul has cried out for more, and I heard it. And I reply, 'Let it be done, because your heart is good'."

A woman in ornate clothes, not at all Jewish, elbows her way through the large crowd. She has a veil over her head and face. She crawls on the ground and kisses the hem of Jesus' garment. She sobs out loud and says, "I am a sinner. I am a prostitute and a killer of babies. Because of my sins, I have incurable diseases. No human doctor can heal me physically, but please heal my soul. I am filth, but I yearn for light. Cure my soul and my body if You wish."

"You are cured, body and soul. Go and sin no more."

The woman again kisses the hem of Jesus' mantle and stands up. In doing so, her veil fails off.

The people shout, "Galatia! Pig! Prostitute! Get out!" and they start throwing rocks and sand at her.

Jesus commands silence. Then He says, "Why do you insult her when she is redeeming herself?"

"She is only redeeming herself because she got sick," they sneer. Turning to the apostles, Jesus says, "Keep her in your midst and get her safely to the boat." The angry crowd turns against Jesus and yells, "False prophet! Protector of prostitutes! Whoever protects them must enjoy them!" They throw dirt and sand at Jesus. He wipes the dirt off His cheek and says, to those who want to defend Him from the mean element in the crowd, "Leave them. I forgive them, and am willing to endure much more for the salvation of a soul."

* * * * *

Am I willing to help someone who is put down by others? Or do I join in the crowd putting that person down? Do I remember that God is willing to forgive any and every sin if the person who committed that sin is sorry? Am I easily swayed by public opinion against an innocent person? Do I value souls as Jesus did?

Activity: Write a friendly letter to someone you know who doesn't feel good about himself or herself. Make the letter upbeat and hope-filled.

Learn the song: "Every Person is a Gift of God," by Carey Landry, Hi God, tape 3.

CHAPTER TWO

Murder of One's Spirit

John of Endor, a Jew, killed the Roman who attempted to abduct his wife. The Romans caught John and put him on a galley ship. He endured three horrible years during which he lost sight in one of his eyes after being hit with a whip.

John knew a lot about herbal medicine, and he made friends with some of the Romans in charge. Finally, the Romans gave John his freedom, but he had become a broken, angry man. He lived in the hills where he got a small chicken farm going, but he didn't trust anyone for fear of being caught again. He sold eggs to the Romans and steered clear of all Jews, even though his unfaithful wife was a Jew.

John read Greek philosophy and poetry, loved his chickens, and stayed away from all human beings as much as possible. Then Jesus came along, and for the first time in his life, John felt loved and forgiven. He gave his neighbor the key to his house and let him have all his chickens. He put on a clean tunic, packed his poetry and other books in a bag, and

set off with Jesus. John had not been so happy in forty years. Then some put-your-nose-in-other-people's-business Jews discovered John was a murderer and began blabbering.

Jesus said later to His apostles, "Yes, they murdered John of Endor with their tongues. It wasn't safe for him to stay in Palestine. John had to leave his homeland and die in faraway Greece. Brothers can be killed in many ways, when as in John's example, persecutors are informed where the persecuted is. But now, they can't hurt John. He is dead. He is happy in heaven. I am happy, too, that he is at peace."

* * * * *

Examine your conscience by asking yourself:

Do I ever hurt people's reputations by spreading bad truths or spreading lies about them?

Do I realize what it means to murder one's spirit?

When I have spoken badly about someone, do I try to undo the damage and make up with that person?

Do I rejoice in the good truths about others? Am I happy about their successes?

Do I remember that when God forgives a person, He doesn't continue digging up the bad stuff?

Activity: Play the telephone game to see how rumors start: the teacher whispers a short sentence in the ear of the first child. It can be said only once. The child relays this sentence to the next child, and the sentence is repeated from child to child in a chain until the last one says what she or he thinks was heard. Compare this with the original information.

CHAPTER THREE

Stephen

Stephen is in the hall of the Jewish Sanhedrin, or priest's court, where they curse him, spit on him, kick him, and grab him by the hair. Blood runs down from his face, but Stephen is calm—he sees something beautiful. He falls on his knees and exclaims, "I see the Son of Man, whom you killed, sitting at the right hand of God."

"Pig! Blasphemer!" they yell, and kick him harder. They bite him, they pick him up by the hair and throw him down. They condemn him to be stoned for following Jesus, and next they drag Stephen out to a barren desert place filled with stones.

A young man named Saul is standing there, with terrible hatred in his face, holding the cloaks of the other men while they hurl stones. As Stephen is struck by the first stones, he remains standing and says to Saul, "My friend, I will wait for you on my way to Christ."

"Pig! Possessed one!" Saul yells, and kicks Stephen so hard he falls over. More stones hit him, mortally injuring him.

Stephen says, "Jesus, receive my spirit. I forgive them." He then crumples up completely. The men keep tossing stones until his body is covered with blood and stones, at which point they leave.

Much later, in the darkness of the night, Peter, James, John, Nicodemus, and the Blessed Virgin Mary, with Lazarus, walk out to where Stephen's body has been left behind. Lazarus carries a little lamp to light the place as they lay Stephen upon a clean cloth. Mary dips a linen cloth into water handed to her by John, and washes the blood off Stephen's face. They dress him in a long tunic, and carry his body away to be buried.

Nicodemus explains that there is a new edict out to kill all Christians. "Let them do what they like," Peter says, "but we will not stop being Christians."

* * * * *

Examine your conscience by asking yourself:

Do I stand up for my faith when others put it down?

Am I afraid to pray before eating in a public restaurant?

As Stephen died for Jesus, am I willing to live for Jesus?

Do I try each day to make some small, hidden sacrifice for Jesus, such as obeying cheerfully, or giving an unpopular person a turn in a game, or helping a younger child with something he or she finds difficult?

Learn the song: "Faith of Our Fathers."

CHAPTER FOUR

A Forgiving Heart

Alphaeus is the brother of Joseph, who is the foster father of Jesus. Alphaeus has four sons; the two younger ones, James and Thaddeus, are among Jesus' followers. When Jesus and His cousins were growing up together, Alphaeus liked Jesus, but after Jesus left home and became an itinerant preacher, Alphaeus considered Jesus insane and didn't want his sons to follow Him.

After praying about it, however, and asking Jesus what was the right thing to do, James and Thaddeus left home and followed Him. Jesus told them it was important to do what God the Father told them, even if their earthly father had other ideas. James and Thaddeus felt sad, because they didn't want their earthly father angry with them, and he was *very* angry and upset.

Now, Alphaeus is older and not well, so Jesus and His apostles plan to visit him and to take some food Alphaeus likes. They carefully pack up fresh eggs, large bunches of grapes, and a big amphora of honey.

Jesus lets James and Thaddeus go ahead to see their father first. When they offer Alphaeus their gifts, he curses them and smashes everything on the kitchen floor. Broken eggs, smashed grapes, and an alabaster jar of honey all mingle in a gooey mess on the floor. Alphaeus yells at them, "You ungrateful sons! You make me the laughing stock of Nazareth by following Jesus! Don't bother to bring me gifts. Go away! The very idea! You make me mad! I don't want you or your gifts!"

Alphaeus stomps out of the room, leaving his two sons crying. Their mother weeps and leans against Jesus, who has just entered through a back door. When she stops crying, Jesus says, "I'll go see Alphaeus now."

"Don't!" his wife pleads. "He has a stick; he'll beat you like he did his own sons. I think he has gone insane!"

"Don't cry, Aunt Mary, I'll be all right." Jesus gently lets her go and goes into the bedroom. Alphaeus yells, "What are *You* doing in here? Are You going to make fun of me, too?"

"No," Jesus replies, "I came to bring you peace. Why are you so cross? Your sons are doing the right thing. You will make yourself more sick by these angry outbursts."

The old man just glares at him. He is visibly shaken and very upset. The Blessed Mother is trying to soothe him. Jesus says, very kindly, "Mother, lift the blankets and we'll make him more comfortable in bed." Mary lifts the blankets, and Jesus pulls the old man up on his pillows so he can breathe easier. Then Jesus says, "Bring some of that hot tea from the fireplace. It will take the chill off him." Mary brings the tea and they help him sip it.

Alphaeus mutters, "Why, why are You so good to me?"

"Because I love you. I've always loved you, and I still do, Uncle."

"I used to love You," Alphaeus mutters, "before You went off preaching and took my two boys."

Jesus repeats, "I love you," and continues, "James and Thaddèus love and follow what God wants of them. You couldn't have two better sons."

"My sons are rebels because of You. Nazareth laughs at me because of You! All because of your stupid folly: You say You are the Messiah, You work miracles. Why don't You work one for me? Cure me and I will forgive You."

"Forgive your sons, and I will give you health."

"Forgive *them*!" the old man cries. "I'll never forgive them. Cursed be both of them! Go tell those serpent sons of mine that I'm dying, and that I'll hold a grudge against them until my dying day!"

"No," Jesus replies. "Don't lose your soul. Do not hate. Call Me insane, if you like, but do not hate. Hate can kill your soul. I love you, Uncle, and I will go on loving you." Jesus leaves the room quietly.

His aunt, in the kitchen, grabs His hand and cries, "Oh Jesus, please forgive him."

"Of course, I forgive him. He is sick. He is old. Grace and your tears and those of James and Thaddeus will work in his heart. Don't be sad, dear Aunt."

Jesus kisses her and leaves.

* * * * *

In your secret place, in the presence of Jesus, examine your conscience by asking yourself:

Do I have a forgiving heart?

Am I willing to forgive?

Do I try to have a heart as kind as Jesus' kind heart?

If I give someone a gift, and that person throws it down

and stomps on it like Alphaeus did, can I still forgive?

Do I ask Jesus to help me forgive?

Do I take time to think what the Act of Love really means—"I forgive all who have injured me and I ask forgiveness of all those whom I have injured"?

Do I take time each night to forgive all of my enemies?

Do I try to think kind thoughts about others?

Do I always ask Jesus to help me forgive? It's not easy, but Jesus will help.

Learn the song: "We Come to Ask Forgiveness," by Carey Landry.

CHAPTER FIVE

Miracle of the Broken Daggers

Jesus crosses a small bridge and goes into a tiny village. Two very angry men are fighting—one man's donkey ate the lettuce from the basket on the back of the other man's donkey. Women scream as the two lunge at each other brandishing short daggers, the blades of which are as wide as your hand.

Jesus yells, "Stop it!" and steps between them. "In the name of God, stop it!"

The men pay Him no attention and keep at each other. "I want to fix this cursed dog once and for all!" the first man yells. The other one screams back, "I'll slice you in two."

Jesus has opened His mantle and holds it up, in between them, like a sheet. They slash holes in His mantle trying to get at each other, yelling, "Get out of our way!"

Nothing seems to calm them. Jesus steps aside and, without a single word, stretches his hands over the daggers. The blades of the daggers fall to the ground in many tiny pieces. The two men stand there, clutching only handles.

Staring at the useless handles, they cease fighting.

"And now, where is your strength?" Jesus asks.

A Roman soldier steps forward and picks up a tiny piece of the shattered dagger, and examines it to see if it is made of real steel. He sees it is, and an expression of amazement comes over his face.

Jesus turns to the crowd and explains how important it is to love one's neighbor and to promote peace.

* * * * *

Jesus turns to you, in your secret place, and asks:

"Do you want to be a leader?" and "Do you want to follow Me?"

"Stand up for truth and justice," He tells you. "Help people to seek peace. Avoid involving yourself in quarrels. Break up fights between others. Do your best to be just, truthful, and peaceful—these are some of the qualities of My leaders. Yes, I invite you. You belong to Me now."

Learn the song: "Go Light Your World" WOW 1996 The Year's 30 Top Christian Artists and Songs (CD ROM).

CHAPTER SIX

Rejection and Rat Spit

"No, you *can't* play! You always mess up *everything*, and besides, we have our teams already chosen," the captain yells.

You stand there, holding your mitt, and then slowly walk away. "Rat spit!" you mutter as you walk off the field. It's after school, and there is no teacher to tell the others that they have to let everyone play.

You slowly head for home. "What a miserable life!" you mutter when you bump into Jesus. He says: "Let's go to your secret place."

"Okay. *Anything* would be better than here!"

You go to your secret place. It's quiet. It's peaceful. No one is there to tell you that you are not wanted on *this* team. Jesus sits down beside you, and says, "Rejection doesn't feel very good." You nod. He goes on: "In fact, no one likes to be rejected, not wanted, put down. Now, let Me ask you a question. What is the best way to handle rejection?"

"Put glue in the pockets of the captain's jacket. That would fix him good."

"How would that fix him?" Jesus asks.

"It would make *me* feel good. I'd get even," you reply.

"How would the captain feel?"

"Bad... exactly what he deserves," you declare.

"Is revenge good?"

"No-o-o, but sometimes a person has to take a stand against unfair people."

"Can you stand up for justice without getting back at them? How about standing up in love?" Jesus suggests.

"How do you do that?" you question Him.

"You love them back, instead of hating. It's tough, but it's Christian. You don't put glue in people's pockets. You don't say mean things. You let the incident go, and when you are captain, you include everyone...."

"Well, I'll have to think this over—it's not easy," you say.

"No, it's never easy to forgive," Jesus responds, and slips away.

* * * * *

You sit there and start praying: "Dear God, that captain makes me so mad I could kill him. I won't, of course, but I'd like to. How can I forgive him? He's so unfair. He's terrible. If You help me, I'll *try* to forgive. I can't promise anything better, but I'll try. I'll *really* try. Help me, God."

CHAPTER SEVEN

Revenge

You go back in time to A.D. 32. Jesus is sitting in a woods, with His back to a large tree, and He is meditating. A twelve-year-old with a herd of goats passes by. One nanny stops beside Jesus and rests her head on His knee. Jesus feeds her a handful of grass and pats her head.

Benjamin, the goatherd boy, comes up to Jesus and begs, "Take me with You, or I'll run away!"

"Why do you want to run away?" Jesus asks kindly, still patting the nanny goat.

"Because Alexander, my master, is cruel," Benjamin cries. "He beats me and starves me. And he won't give me my freedom, even though Eli and two of his friends have already paid for it."

"How do you know they paid?

"Because I was there, but Alexander just says it's his money."

"Can you prove it?"

"Sure—just get Eli and the other two to come and witness."

31

"Eli is an honest man," Jesus says. "Why didn't he do something when Alex wouldn't let you go free?"

"Because Alex is his neighbor, and when he's mad, he takes horrible revenge. Once, a neighbor stood up to Alex, and the next day, all the guy's sheep were dead. Something in the drinking water made them get big bellies and fall over dead—all seventy-five of them."

Jesus stands up. "Let's go talk to Eli, and then you can tell Alex you're free."

"I'm afraid to. Will You go with me?"

"All right," Jesus says.

They go to the woods, where Alex is chopping down a tree. Alex is angry when asked about the situation, and replies: "No, he can't go. He's my servant. That story about the paid ransom is a bunch of lies. May God strike me blind if I don't speak the truth!"

Angrily he throws his ax at Jesus, who ducks. The ax whizzes past Him and chops off a sapling.

Immediately, Alex is blind. He begins to scream. "Take the boy," he howls, "but give me back my sight!"

Jesus says, kindly: "Maybe in the darkness you will see the light." They help Alex back to his house, and Ben puts the goats away. Then he leaves with Jesus and the apostles.

* * * * *

Stop and think:

Do. I take revenge?

Do I keep angry, unforgiving thoughts in my heart?

Do I carry grudges?

CHAPTER EIGHT

Elianna

Jesus and a few of His apostles are walking toward the city when they see an old man staggering along. Jesus says, "Go to that old man with your alms money and buy him some bread."

"We can't," says Peter. "Judas has the purse."

Jesus says, "You are right, Peter. Then, let's look in our bags and give him some bread."

They gather some bread, and Jesus lets the old man drink out of His own water flask. Then Jesus says to him, "Where are you going?"

"To Tekoah," comes the reply.

"Are you alone?" Jesus asks.

"More than alone. My son drove me out of my house...." The man's voice is sad. Jesus says "God will help you, if you believe in Him."

"I do believe in God, and His Messiah. But my son doesn't. He hates the idea of the Messiah so much that he has turned on me, because I love the Messiah. Now he has thrown me out of the house."

"Is that really why he threw you out?" asks Jesus.

"Yes, and also because my son's friends hate the Messiah, and my son doesn't want to lose favor with them. He wanted to show his friends that his hatred was stronger than theirs by throwing out his own father."

"How horrible!" the apostles exclaim.

"It would be even more horrible if I hated my son *and* the Messiah."

"But who *is* your son?" Thomas asks.

"I cannot mention his name—I do not want him despised. I am his father. I am cold and hungry, yet I bear no hatred toward him."

"Since you are a just man, are you not asking anything of God?" Jesus asks gently.

"Yes, that He may touch my son's heart and help him believe in the Messiah."

"But what are you asking for yourself?" Jesus asks.

"That I might meet Him who is, according to me, the Son of God—that I might worship Him, and that I might die…"

Jesus smiles, and the old man continues, "I can't see well, because I am old and hungry, but you are a rabbi, are you not? I think you are a good rabbi."

"Yes, I am a rabbi," Jesus continues. "Have you seen the Master?"

"No, I heard Him in the Temple, but I couldn't see that far."

"You will see Him. God will satisfy you. Where will you stay in Tekoah?" Jesus inquires.

"Under a porch or door; it's all I have now."

"Come with Me. I will take you to an upright Israelite who will receive you." Then Jesus murmurs something quiet to Peter, and Peter hurries off.

When Jesus and the old man are almost to Simon's house, Peter comes back and tells Jesus, "It is done. Simon will take him."

"Come, Father, what is your name?"

"Elianna. My father died before I was born. My mother died giving birth to me. My grandmother brought me up and gave me both my parents' names."

They arrive at the house. "Listen," says Jesus, "Do you want to stay here?"

"Yes, but I want to work. I see no shame in being a servant."

"We shall tell Simon," Jesus says smiling.

The door opens. "Come in, and peace to you!" Simon welcomes them. Basins of warm water are brought to wash their feet.

Elianna objects, "You must not wash my feet; I came to serve."

Simon replies, "We will find a job for you. First, you must be refreshed and have something to eat."

Elianna looks Jesus over carefully and exclaims, "You are the most high God!" and he bows before Him.

Jesus hugs Elianna and says, "You have given more than I have given you. You have given much love."

* * * * *

Examine your conscience by asking yourself:

Do I let go of grudges and pray for the person who has hurt me?

Do I refuse to gossip about people who have hurt me? (Remember, Elianna wouldn't even give the name of his son!)

Do I put Jesus ahead of other concerns?

Art: Draw symbol-pictures of times you have been hurt (for instance, someone made fun of your picture of a horse, so now you draw a small horse. Second example: someone called you an idiot. You print "idiot." Now, after you have several symbols drawn, you go through each one and tell Jesus you forgive the persons who did them. Then you tear up the pictures into tiny pieces and ask Jesus to help you let go of all the bad feelings— to take them away completely. Then you thank God for the gift of forgiveness.

CHAPTER NINE

The Power of Forgiveness

Dominic was scarcely nineteen when the Nazis captured him in Holland and took him to a concentration camp in Germany. He and the other men with him suffered dreadfully from cold, endured beatings, and had little food. Dominic's six-foot frame went from a healthy 160 pounds to ninety. He saw men grab live wires around the camp to end the misery of their lives.

Dominic, a good Catholic, wondered: "Does God really exist? If so, why does He let this go on?" He tried not to doubt, but he couldn't help it. He prayed every night that God would help him seek good, not evil.

After the war, when he was released, Dominic forgave the Nazis, married his childhood sweetheart in Holland, and came to the United States. He was a beautiful, gentle, compassionate man, fully Christian. His five grown children are wonderful Christians, too.

Can I forgive? Suppose, like Dominic, I were to suffer life-long effects from the Nazis' prison camp—could I forgive?

When someone steals my mitt, do I forgive? When my little sister "borrows" my marker pens and wrecks the whole set, do I forgive? When my dad yells at me for something my brother did, do I forgive? When my parents expect me to be in by eleven o'clock and the other kids get to stay out until midnight, do I forgive?

Remember, we all need help.

* * * * *

Song: "We Come To Ask Forgiveness," Carey Landry.

—This true story was used with permission. Dominic died in June 1993 of a heart attack.

"Seek good and not evil, That you may live...."
AMOS 5:14

CHAPTER TEN

Marjiam

Marjiam is a young Jewish boy who, at age ten, lost his parents, his brother, and his sister in a landslide. He was with his grandfather at the time and escaped injury. His grandfather, Simon, is a servant for a rich, mean Pharisee, Doras, who gives his workers very little food and makes them work long hours in the fields.

At this time, Mary, the Mother of Jesus, has Marjiam with her and is teaching him to pray to Our Father. "But can God, who is good, love Doras, who is so bad and makes my old grandfather weep?" he asks.

"God loves Doras and wants him to repent," Mary replies. "You must pray that Doras repents."

"Hardly, Mother! I will pray that he may die!" cries Marjiam.

"Oh, no, you must help a sinner. Life is good, because it gives a person a chance to repent and gain merit," Mary says to him.

"But if one is bad, one gains sins," Marjiam reasons.

"We must pray that he will become good," Mary says.

"Doras is so bad, he won't become good even if I pray for him. You know, one day he struck my grandfather with an iron rod because he found him sitting down instead of working. Grandfather was so sick he couldn't stand up.

Doras beat him and left him half-dead. Blood was all over his beard, and then Doras kicked him in the face," Marjiam tells Mary. "I was weeping so hard, I had to hide in the woods, or he would have beaten me, too. I was without any bread for two days. I would like to beat Doras so he knows how it feels. I would like to make him work in the rain, the mud, and the sun without food, so he knows how it feels. I cannot love him, because he kills my holy father."

Marjiam cries, "I cannot forgive him. I hate him!"

He strikes the air with clenched fists and screams again, "I hate him!"

Jesus comes over and puts His hand on Marjiam's shoulder. He turns to Mary and says, "That was Doras' worst sin—to drive an innocent child to hate." Then Jesus takes Marjiam in His arms and says, "Listen, do you someday want to be with your mother, father, sister, brother and grandfather?"

"Yes," Marjiam admits.

"Then you must not hate *anyone*. He who hates does not go to heaven. You cannot pray for Doras now, but you must pray to God for help and try not to look back. Tell God in heaven how much you love your old grandfather and how much you love all those who are unhappy. Then ask God to please take care of everything. Leave things to God. Do not hate. Try to forgive. Will you do that?" Jesus asks Marjiam.

"Yes I will, because I love You."

Jesus kisses the boy and sets him down.

* * * * *

Examine your conscience by asking yourself:
When someone wrongs me, do I immediately lash out

in hate?

Do I try to forgive even if I feel angry?

Do I ask God for help? None of us can forgive by our own power.

Do I stand up for justice without being vengeful? Do I hang onto past grudges?

Do I bury the hatchet, but then carefully mark the spot so I can dig it up again?

Do I say the Act of Love—"I forgive all who have injured me and ask pardon of all whom I have injured"— and mean it?

Song: "We Come to Ask Forgiveness," Carey Landry.

CHAPTER ELEVEN

The Quality of Mercy

You are in the eighth grade and your grandparents have given you a CD player. Your mom tells you to keep your bedroom door locked while you are at school, because your little brother Benjamin, nicknamed Bugsy, gets into things.

One day, you forget to lock the door. Bugsy gets in and chews up your favorite CD. In fact, he does more than chew it: he bites out a big hunk. You come home and find the mess. You are angry. You find him playing in the backyard and you hold up the mutilated disk. "Look at this!" you start yelling, and then you give him a whack on the rear end. He starts to cry. Your mom steps out: "What's going on here?"

"Look at this!" you yell again.

"Yes, I see—it's ruined," she says.

"And I don't have any money to get a new one," you point out, "and I promised the guys I'd play it at Joe's party tomorrow night."

"I'll see if I can replace it tomorrow, but I'm not sure I can get one that fast. You mustn't hit Bugsy. Let me correct him," your mother tells you.

"Why can't he stay out of my stuff? Baby brothers are such a pain!" you moan.

"*You* were little once, too," Mom reminds you. "Remember the time you dumped two pounds of nails into Dad's open paint can? Your father was so angry, it was a week before he could talk to you...."

"I remember," you mutter. "That was a long time ago."

Your mom goes back to the kitchen. You go back to your room to see if there is any other damage. Two torn books and one wrecked compact disk. You sit on the edge of your bed with your chin in your hands.

Then Jesus sits down next to you and says, very gently: "Forgive Bugsy."

"Rat Spit! I can't!" you mutter. "I'd like to beat him."

"No, that won't help. Come to your secret place and sit awhile," Jesus invites you. "Let My Spirit speak to your heart."

"What good will *that* do?" you wonder.

"It will help you understand mercy," Jesus tells you.

"I don't want mercy—I want justice!" you exclaim.

"True justice and mercy go hand in hand. You must forgive," Jesus advises you, "or you will carry a burden like a ton of bricks on your back. It will weigh you down... you must forgive."

"How can I forgive that little brat?" you cry.

"Didn't your father forgive you when you put those nails in that new paint?" Jesus asks very gently.

"Yes, but not right away. My mom pleaded with him for a week, and I didn't get to play with neighbor kids for two weeks."

"Just sit still and pray to feel forgiveness."

You sit still and mutter, "God, help me to forgive Bugsy. I feel very angry. He had no business in my room. I'd like to beat Bugsy, but I know that wouldn't help. God, why is it so hard to forgive? Jesus, how did You manage to forgive those who hung You on the cross? I just don't understand it all. Please help me. I'm willing to try, but I can't promise anything."

CHAPTER TWELVE

Dog Days

Jesus walks up to you and says, "Come quickly to our secret place." You drop your soccer ball and go. Jesus continues, "I want you to imagine forty families in this little town who have a pet dog. Imagine big dogs, little dogs, furry dogs, slick dogs, black dogs, spotted dogs, all kinds—friendly dogs, mean dogs, *every possible kind*. Now imagine these forty dogs have gone berserk—they mess the carpet, they tear up easy chairs, they fight. They bite little children. Now, they run outside in a big pack, like angry wolves. Frenzied, they attack a three-year-old. The paramedics come and sadly shake their heads. "It's too late," they say as they tenderly lay the child on a stretcher.

Jesus continues, "I know you like dogs. You are an animal lover, and it makes you sad to see how bad these dogs behave. I want you to help these dogs act better, but to do it, you have to become a dog. What kind do you want to be?"

"Any kind You want," you say to Jesus. "I think I'll be a honey-colored collie."

Jesus blesses you and you become a collie. "Now you can help those dogs become tame again," Jesus says.

You run down the road and join the pack. They snarl. They fight. They chew the ears off a smaller terrier. You speak in dog language to a mean-looking German shepherd and say, "Don't be so mean to that little fox terrier."

"You wanna make something of it?" he snarls, baring his teeth. You step back because you don't want *your* ears chewed off.

You run with the dogs for three months. Some get a little better, but many get worse. One group hates you because you don't do any bad-dog stuff. One day, this group has a meeting. They don't invite you, but they make plans for your destruction. You hear about their plans from a toy terrier who snuck up on the edge of the group and listened as they said, "He's just too good. We better kill him."

"How?" asked a pit bull.

"Tear him to pieces," another dog suggested.

"We have enough dogs to do it," replied the German shepherd.

You feel bad. "What do I do now? I've only helped a few, and these others are out for my blood!" you tell Jesus when you have rushed back to your secret place before the pack can catch you. "I want whatever advice You can give to change those dogs' behavior."

"You forgive and offer your life to the Father. Your life is the biggest gift."

You sit quietly and think, *am I brave enough to give my life? Jesus was.*

But can you redeem them? This is a big order. How much love will it take to give your life for them? And then what if it doesn't change them?

* * * * *

Learn the song: "If I Were a Butterfly," Carey Landry.

CHAPTER THIRTEEN

Light Baggage

"Why do we have to move, Mom?" asks thirteen-year-old Cindy as she carefully packs her best blouses.

"Because Dad's new job is in Texas. And with jobs hard to get, we have to take it," is her mom's answer.

"But I don't want to leave my friends…!" wails Cindy.

"Neither do I," replies her Mom, "but there's nothing we can do. We'll just have to find new friends."

"I guess so," mumbles Cindy, arranging her books in a big box. She flips open her newest birthday book and reads the inscription her grandmother wrote on the title page: "Remember, wherever you go, you take my love with you."

"Grandma," she whispers, "I sure will." And the packing doesn't seem so tedious after that.

* * * * *

Jesus sits down by you in your secret place and says, "Remember: there are many things you can't take with you,

but love is one that you can."

"Yes," you reply, "I'll remember that."

Ask yourself, do I carry too much baggage?

Is my room cluttered with shoes, toys, clothes, puzzles, and balls that I will never use?

Could I share the things I don't need and that are still good with someone less fortunate?

Can I remember to always carry love in my heart?

Can I remember that where there is love, there will be no room for grudges, anger, and resentment?

Can I remember that it pays to travel light?

CHAPTER FOURTEEN

The Beggar Olga

Jesus is eating bread and olives in the side square of a small town. A ragged beggar approaches Jesus and asks for a little bread. Jesus gives him all He has.

"What about You?" Peter asks. "We have no money to buy food. We gave everything to Ananias."

"It's all right. I am not hungry, just thirsty."

The beggar says to Jesus, "There is a well in back of the village. I will take You there. But if You want, I'll give You back some bread to eat, if you are not disgusted taking from a beggar."

Jesus says, "Go ahead and eat it, but to show you I'm happy to receive from a beggar, I'll take one portion." The beggar smiles and gives him back some bread and olives. Ogla is so pleased. He asks, "What is Your name?"

"Jesus of Nazareth, the rabbi of Galilee."

"Are You not the Messiah?"

"I am."

"And You are so good to beggars! You do not beat us

like the Tetrarch when he wants us out of the way."

"I am the Savior. I do not beat—I love."

The man stares at Jesus and begins slowly to weep.

"Why are you weeping?" Jesus inquires of Ogla.

"Because I would like to be saved. I have sinned. I need help... I could take You to the well for a drink?"

"I'm coming, too!" Peter cries.

"No, you stay here. I'm going with Ogla alone. He wants to talk privately." Jesus takes the man behind some trees.

Ogla says, "The well is over there. We'll get Your drink first."

"No, speak what is in your heart, and I will perhaps have my thirst satisfied," Jesus urges him.

"We were seven brothers born of one father, but I was born of my father's second wife after his first died. I was hated by my brothers, who drove my mother and me out after my father died. Then they bribed the judges and took our inheritance. My mother died of starvation when I was sixteen.

"From that day on, I cursed and hated my brothers. When five of them died after living rich lives, the last living brother got all the goods. I hated him more than ever. And one day he met me at the market, and insulted and beat me. I vowed to get even.

"One evening, I met him alone by the river. He was intoxicated with wine, and I was intoxicated with hate. I was twenty-six. He insulted my mother by calling her a bitch. I caught him by the neck, intending just to beat him. We struggled on the slippery grass. He slipped and went down the ravine. The swift river took him. They are still looking for him. I didn't intend to kill him," he sobs. "I'm afraid to die and afraid to live."

"I am mercy," Jesus says, "not terror. I will take those sins on Me. Do you want forgiveness?"

"For what? Of killing my brother?"

"You killed six brothers by hating and cursing them..." Jesus tells Ogla.

"I offered sacrifices at the Temple," Ogla says, "but I do not know if they were accepted."

"They were not. You must be sorry and make up for these sins. Go to My disciples and shepherds. Tell them I sent you. Live to make up for this," directs Jesus.

"But you didn't get a drink!" Ogla cries.

"I have drunk your tears. To Me, a soul returning to God is more important," Jesus replies.

"So I am forgiven?"

"Yes, go in peace."

* * * * *

Examine your conscience: ask yourself, am I really sorry for any mean things I've done to others—name-calling, fighting, cruel words, anger?

Do I hold grudges?

Do I refuse to speak to someone who has hurt me?

Am I kind in my thoughts?

When I have forgiven, do I try not to go back over the bad stuff?

Do I understand that God will always help me to be reconciled with my peers and others, if I ask?

Do I try to forgive, as Jesus does, from the heart?

CHAPTER FIFTEEN

Decapolis Demoniac

Jesus and His apostles are walking along when they are approached by some men who say, "Nothing can cure him. He is totally possessed by Satan. He runs around naked and terrifies women."

"How awful!" some of the apostles comment.

"Yes, he got hold of a girl who was coming back from the river, and she died of a high temperature after being grabbed by that man," says one of the group.

"Yes, and I'll tell you what else," says another. "My brother-in-law was fixing the tomb because his father-in-law died, and that demoniac was in there throwing rocks at him. My brother-in-law had to run back to the village or he'd be dead."

Jesus listens. The men go on talking. "Remember when Daniel and Tobias tied him up and took him by force to his home? Later, when they were in their new boat, he turned the boat upside down, broke the oars, and ruined the boat. They lost everything and had to swim fast for their lives."

"Yes, it's a terrible curse to have that demon around. When he was tied up and taken to the priests in the Temple, they couldn't do a thing because—"

"Because what?" asks Jesus. "Go ahead, I won't accuse you."

"Well, the high priest might be successful if he were a..." the man's voice trails off.

"A holy man?" Jesus finishes the thought.

"Yes, that's right. I didn't want to say it, but You can cure him. You *are* a holy man. You are the Son of God."

Jesus asks, "How do you know?"

"Last year, we saw You stop the river at high tide in a winter storm. Only God can do that. Will You cure this demoniac? Please?"

They keep on walking.

A voice yells, "Go away! I'll kill you! Get back!"

The people with Jesus stop. Jesus keeps on walking.

"Go away! I will kill You. Stop persecuting me!" The madman rolls on the ground bites himself, jumps up and points his finger at Jesus. Jesus orders, "Be silent, demon of this man, I order you!"

"No! Leave me alone!" he yells. "Why can't You leave me alone? I hate You. I want to curse You, but I can't."

Jesus comes closer, about three feet from the man, and orders, "Come out of him. I command you to come out!"

"No!" the demon roars.

"In the name of God, come out!" Jesus commands.

"Why do You defeat me?"

Jesus says, "Who are you?"

"I am Beelzebub, the head of all the devils." The demoniac becomes stiff and motionless. Jesus spreads His arms wide and orders, "Come out, Satan!"

The man makes a long cry, "AA-a-a-hhhh!" and cries, "I am coming out. You have defeated me!"

There is loud crash, and a huge tree falls over, but there is no thunder or lightning. The madman falls over on the ground. Jesus reaches down and takes the man's hand. "Don't be afraid."

The people approach. Jesus says, "Bring some clothes." They run to get some. The man sits up and wipes blood, foam, and perspiration from his face. Then he realizes he is naked and says,"What happened? Who are You? Why am I here without my clothes on?"

Before anyone can answer his questions, the clothes arrive and they dress him. An old woman arrives, weeping, "Son, you are cured."

"Who cured me?" the man asks in a daze.

"Jesus of Nazareth. His name is goodness. Bless His name and thank Him."

"Be good now," Jesus says, "Obey the commandments." The man looks embarrassed.

The angry Pharisees come up and sneer at Jesus. "Sure, he got rid of the demon because Jesus is the master of demons."

The man's mother angrily replies, "You mean, cruel ones. You have no mercy or respect!"

Jesus says, "Don't bother about them. Be happy with your son. The Pharisees don't worry Me. I am truth."

Then Jesus goes off with His apostles and explains to them the three main ways by which a person becomes possessed: sensuality (lack of purity), love of money, and pride of spirit. Jesus explains how important it is not to let any of these have a foothold in one's heart, but to keep oneself open to God.

* * * * *

Do I let Satan into my life in little ways? By lying? Stealing? Telling half-truths? Looking at inappropriate images in magazines, on the Internet or television?

Do I really want to be clean of heart? Am I tempted to think too much of money and what money can buy?

Sit still and ask Jesus to help you to be clean of heart, free from avarice, and free from the wrong kind of pride.

Art: Make a chart with three columns on a large piece of drawing paper. In the first column, draw things—e.g., money, cars, heart, people, etc. In the second column, show a bad use of this; in the third column, show a good use.

CHAPTER SIXTEEN

Touched by God

The innkeeper is sad. He speaks to Philip: "I have a daughter. She is a lunatic. She remains like a mute animal. Do you think Jesus can cure her?"

"Yes, He can," Philip reassures him. "You must believe. I have seen Him drive out many demons. At Gerasenes, they went into the pigs. I am a witness to His power."

"All right. Please call Jesus to help me."

Andrew, who is standing there, says, "I will go myself," and he runs off. He sees Jesus in the marketplace. "Come quickly, the innkeeper's daughter is insane. A demon has gotten into her. The man is begging for Your help."

Jesus asks, "Does he know Me?"

"We have tried to make You known," Andrew replies.

"And you have." Jesus smiles. "Let's go."

Together, they go to the inn. A big crowd is there. When the innkeeper sees Jesus, he rushes over and kneels down. "Have mercy on my daughter. I have sinned by cheating people, but don't take it out on her. Forgive me and help me."

Jesus says, "Stand up, and take Me to your daughter."

"She is in the stable and won't come out," the innkeeper tells Jesus.

"It doesn't matter. I'll go to her." They enter the dark stable, where the girl cowers in the back corner. She shouts, "Go back. Leave me alone! You are the Christ."

Jesus commands, "Go out of this girl. Give her back to God. I command it now!"

The girl screams, then collapses on the straw floor. Her skin is deathly pale; then color slowly returns to her face. She sits up quietly and says, "Where am I? What happened?" She looks down at her torn, dirty clothing and feels embarrassed. A big crowd is watching her.

Her father weeps and hugs her. Her mother squeezes through the crowd and kisses her. The people shout in amazement, "Truly, He is the Son of God!"

The innkeeper says, "Stay with us, Jesus, it's getting dark!"

Jesus replies, "Man, we are thirteen."

"Even if you were 300, I would feed and house you. Thank you! Thank you!"

* * * * *

Jesus sits down by you, in your secret place, and says, "Tell Me about a time when you were touched by God—a time when you felt that God was really close, a time when you wanted to do your very best for God.

"Think about this innkeeper. Think about how grateful he is to have his oldest. daughter cured. Remember some favor you are grateful for and thank God. Try today to look for what is good and true and beautiful in people, and in the world."

Activity: Listen to this song, "Let Not Your Heart Be Troubled," by Sister Marianne Misetich, SNJM; think about how the innkeeper was troubled, and how Jesus helped him. How can you help people?

CHAPTER SEVENTEEN

Faith in the Love of God

Jesus is speaking in a place called Clear Water. A woman approaches with her son, who was badly injured when he was run over by a heavy wagon. She carries her little boy on a board; both of his legs were fractured and his back has been broken.

"Doctors can't fix him," the mother says through her tears. "He will have to lie on his back all his life."

Jesus looks at the little boy and asks him, "Is it very painful?"

"Yes, it's very bad. It hurts all the time," says the boy.

"Where does it hurt?" Jesus wants to know.

"Here... and here," he groans, pointing to his lower back.

Jesus says, "Shall I take you in My arms?"

"Yes," responds the little boy, with longing in his voice.

"Come, then."

"But Master!" the mother cries, "It hurts too much—he can't move. The doctor said he would never move—"

"I will not hurt him. I am not the doctor," Jesus asserts.

60

"I am Who am. Do you believe in Me?"

"*Yes*—I believe You are the Messiah."

"Come, then." Jesus nods to the boy, puts one arm under his shoulders and one under his legs, and picks him up. "We will go up front and talk to the people."

The little boy smiles and shows no pain. Jesus, carrying the boy, takes a seat on a platform the apostles have set up, and begins speaking to the people about observing the Sabbath.

He asks the little boy resting across His knees, "Do you like this?"

"Oh, yes, it's very nice," The boy plays with Jesus' beard and twines his fingers in one long lock of hair. Then he goes to sleep, still holding the lock of hair.

Jesus says, "The little boy followed the look of love on My face. What a beautiful child! Now, I will wake him up with a kiss." Jesus kisses the top of his head and the child wakes up. Jesus asks, "What is your name?"

"John," he tells Him.

"Do you want to walk? So, you want to run to your mother and say: 'The Messiah blesses you because you believed'?"

"Yes—oh, yes! I'd like that!" Then John says, "Will I be able to walk in the meadow? No more boards? No more doctors?"

"Yes, no more boards, no more doctors ever again," promises Jesus.

"Oh, how I love You!" John throws his arms around Jesus' neck and kisses Him. Then, to reach Him better, he kneels on Jesus' knees and showers Him with kisses.

The crowd begins shouting. John turns to Jesus and asks, "Why are they yelling?"

"They are happy that you can walk."

John runs to his mother and kisses her. "Why are you crying, Mama?"

"Because I'm so happy!" She gives him a big hug and kiss.

Jesus turns to the crowd and says, "Have faith in the love of God, as little John did, and go in peace."

* * * * *

Examine your conscience by asking yourself:

Am I compassionate with those who are suffering?

Do I have time for them?

Am I kind? Am I caring? Am I gentle?

Think about how, today, you can help someone.

CHAPTER EIGHTEEN

The Man from Jabneel

Jesus is walking along the road when he sees what looks like a bundle of rags. The bundle turns out to be a man, half-dead, but still breathing.

Jesus bends over him and asks, "Are you sick?"

"Yes," comes the very faint response.

"Why did you set out in this state?" Jesus wants to know. "Don't you have any relatives or friends?"

The man nods, too weak to answer. Jesus says, "If I supported you, do you think you could make it to that village?"

The man shakes his head, and two big tears roll down his hollow cheeks. "The people drove me out. They thought I had leprosy," he tells Jesus, "but I don't." He pulls some green shoots out of his mouth. "I've been living on green corn. It doesn't keep me."

Jesus says, "I'm going to get some milk from that shepherd." He goes to the hillside and approaches the shepherd for a bowl of milk. At first, the shepherd hesitates, and then he unhooks a bowl hanging from his belt. He milks a goat. "Here You are," he

offers the bowl to Jesus.

Jesus thanks him, and takes the milk to the dying man while the shepherd looks on. Jesus says, "Just take a little sip, and then rest. Your stomach can't handle much yet." The man closes his eyes and waits. Gradually, he recovers a little strength. He smiles his gratitude and says, "I'm making You lose time."

Jesus replies, "Time spent loving one's brother is never lost. When you feel better, we will talk."

"I *am* feeling better. My body is coming alive. I thought I would die here without seeing my five children again. My wife is dead. My mother-in-law is caring for my children."

"Rest now. Take it easy," Jesus says to the man, who tells Him, "I wish I could go to Ephraim."

Jesus asks, "Do you come from Ephraim?"

"No, from Jabneel. I have an incurable disease. Although I am not a Jew, I wanted to reach the rabbi of Galilee to get cured. A friend told me the rabbi helps all people. My friend told me the rabbi is as good as He is powerful. And I believe it. My friend said He was at Ephraim. I had to sell my donkey, because I ran out of money. My friend said the rabbi is the Messiah."

"Do you believe it?"

"Yes, and I believe He is the Son of God. Perhaps You can take me to Him? Perhaps You are one of His disciples?"

Jesus smiles and says, "Try Me out. Ask Me to cure you."

"You are a good man. There is much peace in You. I believe You can cure me," the man tells Jesus, "but I want my *soul* cured. I want to be a just man. Only the rabbi can do that. I want my soul to live."

"If you believe and ask for a miracle, you will have it."

The man kneels, with difficulty, and says, "Jesus, Son of

God, have mercy on me!"

"Let it be done as your faith deserves!" Jesus says, blessing him. The man is dazzled, and utters a shrill cry. He falls over on the grass.

The shepherd comes running. "Is he dead? More than milk is needed when a man is that far gone!"

The man hears him, stands up, and cries, "Dead? I am a new man! I am cured. I feel like I did the day I was married! Oh, blessed Jesus—why didn't I recognize You?" He throws himself before Jesus and worships Him.

* * * * *

Jesus turns to you and says, "Think about this: The time spent in loving one's brother is never lost."

Examine your conscience by asking yourself:

Have I gone out of my way to help someone today?

Have I made any bad judgments about people today?

Am I willing to take time for people?

Do I pull back when my parents ask me to do something extra?

Do I understand that it is good to have one's body cured, but it is more important to have one's soul cured?

Am I willing to take the time that is needed to develop spiritually?

Learn the song: "Living and Loving and Learning," Carey Landry.

CHAPTER NINETEEN

MYOB

W hy do I have to do *everything* around here?" complains Lisa as she empties the dishwasher. "You don't," her mother replies. "Everyone has a job."

"Oh, yeah, yeah, but they don't *do* them. When did Joe last cut the grass? Has Ellen fed the dog lately? I saw Toby do it last week…"

Her mother bites her lip and replies, "Since when is it *your* business to check on everyone? All you have to do is empty the dishwasher, and then MYOB."

＊ ＊ ＊ ＊ ＊

Jesus says, "Now, you must come to your secret place and think about these things."

Ask yourself:

Do I complain?

Do I compare my jobs with the jobs of everyone else in the house?

Do I constantly hassle my parents about fairness?

Am I fair in my judgments?

Do I realize each person has a different gift?

Am I compassionate and willing to be merciful?

Do I go around looking for trouble?

Do I do my part to make the family atmosphere loving and happy?

Learn the song: "God Has Made Us A Family," Carey Landry.

*MYOB= Mind Your Own Business.

CHAPTER TWENTY

Kindness to Orphans

J esus is on His way to the house of Jacob, a rich farmer, when He sees two children—a girl about eight years old and a boy of about four—shabbily dressed and very hungry-looking. The children hang back behind the corner of Jacob's house, trying to find shelter from the cold and biting wind. Jesus and His apostles open the gate and go toward the rich man's house.

"Come in," Jacob says. "You are welcome!" Then he spots the children, at whom he yells, "Go away, you filthy brats! There is nothing here for you. You are probably thieves."

"Have mercy," the girl says. "How about a piece of bread for my brother? We are hungry."

Jesus says, "Who is it that is hungry?"

"I, sir, my brother and I," replies the girl. "Just a piece of bread, and we will go away."

"Come here," Jesus says kindly.

"I am afraid, sir," the girl tells Him.

"Come, I tell you." Jesus reaches out to the two children. "Do not be afraid of Me."

The girl comes out from behind the corner of the house. Her brother clutches the sleeve of her ragged dress. She looks timidly at Jesus, and with fear at Jacob.

Jacob gives them a nasty look and says to Jesus, "They are vagabonds and thieves. I saw them scraping near my oil mill. They were probably trying to steal something."

Jesus gazes at the ragged girl and hungry boy. "Is it true that you wanted to steal? Tell Me. Do not be afraid."

"No, sir, I only asked for a little bread and they wouldn't give me any. I saw an oily crust on the ground and was going to pick it up. Oh, why didn't they put us into the grave with our mother?" the little girl weeps.

"Do not weep," Jesus caresses her. "When did your mother die?"

"A month ago, and Father died at harvest time."

"Who was his master?"

"Ishmael. He sent us away. He said the street was the place for starving dogs. We have no relatives," the girl sobs.

Jesus turns to Jacob. "And you, Jacob—why did you not give them any bread and a little milk?"

"Because they are like stray animals: if you feed them, they won't go away. I have just enough for myself."

"Can you *truthfully* say that? You have rich crops, much oil and fruit. You will see a new miracle. And when it comes, remember to beat your chest and say, 'I deserved that'. How can you refuse two starving children?" Jesus turns to the children and directs them, "Go to that tree and pick the fruit."

"But it is bare, sir," objects the girl.

"Go," Jesus says kindly. The girl goes and comes back

with her apron full of red apples. Jesus says, "Eat of them and then come with Me."

Jesus takes the two orphans to Johanna, a widow lady who receives them warmly, feeds them, and shelters them.

* * * * *

In your secret place, in the presence of Jesus, examine your conscience by asking yourself:

How do I treat others?

Am I kind to children who don't have the best clothes? Do I put down children who have less spending money than I?

Do I make fun of others when they make mistakes in class? Do I put others down? Am I cruel in teasing?

Do I show respect and kindness?

Learn the song: "Whatsoever You Do," by Willard F Jabusch, OCP.

CHAPTER TWENTY-ONE

Helping the Underdog

Annaleah, a young and beautiful woman, is engaged to be married. She becomes ill with an incurable disease. Her fiancé is sad. Jesus cures her, and then both the young man and woman are very happy.

But as Annaleah becomes strong again, she changes her mind about getting married. She wants to follow Jesus instead. She explains this to her boyfriend, who is a bit upset, but he lets her go where her heart is. Annaleah reads the Scriptures and knows that Jesus has to suffer and to die; so she begs Him to take her to heaven before this can happen, and He does. Annaleah is perfectly healthy, and then suddenly dies when she is eighteen years old.

Annaleah's mother, Eliza, is upset at losing her only daughter, but being a woman of faith, she believes Annaleah will be in heaven to greet her when she dies.

Then, shortly after Jesus' resurrection, one early morning, Eliza is weeping in her daughter's room. She kneels on the floor, with her head on the unmade bed, when Jesus enters

the room and asks, "Why are you weeping, Eliza?"

"Because yesterday, the men said Jesus was nothing and that the apostles had stolen away His body. And I'm sorry my daughter died to be with Him—maybe it's all a hoax..." She doesn't lift her head, so Eliza can't realize it is Jesus to whom she is speaking.

"But many have seen Him risen," she hears her companion say.

"I told them that, and no one believes me," she replies, and begins weeping louder, still without looking up.

"If you saw the risen Lord and touched Him," Jesus inquires, "would you believe?"

"Women can't touch the Holy of Holies," Eliza sobs, "but if I saw Him, I would believe—oh, I would!"

"Look up, Eliza, and see who is standing in front of you," Jesus says to her.

Eliza lifts up her tear-stained face and then falls to her heels to worship Jesus. She is so amazed that she opens her mouth, but no words come out.

"It is I," Jesus smiles. "Have faith. You sacrificed your only daughter to Me. Kiss My hand and know that I am your Jesus."

"Oh, You *are* really risen! I knew it!" Eliza exclaims. "But so many put You down. I *do* believe! I'm happy now!"

Jesus disappears then in a great light, and Eliza kneels in prayerful wonderment.

* * * * *

In your secret place, in the presence of Jesus, examine your conscience by asking yourself:

How many times do I let people around me put others down?

Do I stand up for the underdog?

Am I kind in my thoughts and words?

Am I afraid of what people think?

Help me today, Jesus, to stand up for those who can't help themselves.

Learn the song: "They'll Know We Are Christians," Peter Scholtes, OCP.

CHAPTER TWENTY-TWO

Eli's Grandson Suffers Snakebite

Jesus and His apostles are just getting off Peter's boat when Eli comes running, yelling, "Mercy, forgive Me, Jesus. I have spoken badly of You, but I need You now. Please help my grandson—he is dying from a snakebite!" Eli weeps and strikes his head on the ground.

Jesus says, "Come on! Let's go take care of him."

"But, do you know who I am?" Eli wonders.

"An unhappy man," Jesus notes. "Let's go."

Peter says, "Lord, do You think You can change his heart? Why waste time on an enemy? Let the little snake die, and maybe the big snake will come around."

"Simon Peter! *You* are the snake now," Jesus says, and goes to the four-year-old in the arms of his mother. The little child's head is drooping, and he looks half dead. His thumb is blue from the snakebite. His grandfather does nothing but howl, "Jesus, Jesus!"

Jesus takes the boy's hand and sucks the venom from the wound, spitting it away. Then He blesses the waxy little

face and half-open eyes, and says, "The child will now get well." Color comes back to the boy's face. He yawns and opens his eyes, then startles as he remembers the snake and wriggles, trying to get away. He falls into the arms of Jesus, who says, "Don't be afraid—you're all right now. See the beautiful sun on the trees?"

"Where is the snake?" the little boy asks suspiciously.

"He's gone," Jesus replies, "but I'm here now."

"You, yes—you. Grandfather told me to curse you, but I won't. I love you—I do," and he gives Jesus a big hug.

"I never said that!" Eli yells. "He's raving! Don't pay any attention!"

Jesus looks Eli straight in the eye and replies calmly, "Words are not always of value. Love one another if you can, and always speak the truth." Then Jesus turns and leaves.

* * * * *

Examine your conscience by asking yourself:

Am I ever two-faced? Do I say one thing when I mean another?

Do I ever mislead younger children?

Am I kind? Am I truthful?

Do I try to help younger children?

Art: Draw three cartoon pictures. Use stick figures if you like. Label each picture carefully. Show an image of a child your age helping a younger child.

For fast workers: Draw a picture of Eli's grandson and the snake.

CHAPTER TWENTY-THREE

Double Fruit

Jesus and His apostles are on the border of Samaria, going through a wheat field. They are trying not to attract attention, because the Pharisees have been giving Jesus a bad time, and Jesus knows the time has not yet come when He is to be caught and put to death.

Ten lepers come charging down from above the wheat field, shouting, "Jesus, Rabbi, Master, Son of David! Have mercy on us!"

Peter says, "Let's get out of here—we don't want the whole village following us!"

Jesus looks at the lepers and asks them, "Are you from this village?"

"No," they reply, "we are from all over."

Jesus replies, "Go to the nearest village and show your-selves to the high priests." Jesus blesses them and keeps on walking.

Peter says, "You did the right thing in not curing them. We don't want the whole village on our tail." Jesus says nothing,

but keeps on walking. Then a loud voice breaks the stillness: "Praise to God most high! He is full of wisdom and mercy! He has given me health! Jesus is truly God! I glorify Him!"

"Be quiet!" Peter shouts. "We are trying to get of here without a following!"

The man replies, "But Jesus healed me! I need to bless Him and thank Him."

"Well then, do it quietly in your heart! We don't want anyone following us just now."

"Sorry, I cannot be quiet! May God be praised! May Jesus reign forever! Salvation has come!"

Peter shrugs and turns away. The healed leper goes on bellowing his praise. Peter turns to Jesus, who says, "I will dismiss him." He calls the leper over. The man bows down.

"Stand up! Were not ten made clean? And only a Samaritan returns to give thanks? Go in the light, and may my Heavenly Father reward you."

The man kisses the ground in front of Jesus and says, "Give me a new name. I am a new man. Everything in me is new."

Jesus tells him, "You will be Ephrem, which means 'Double fruit!'" The man goes away, smiling and praising God.

* * * * *

Do I remember to say "Thank You" for little things? For big things?

When I am cleansed from the leprosy of sin in confession, do I say, "Thank You, God"?

Do I take time to thank my parents for food, for new clothes, for love, for being there?

Do I thank Jesus at Mass for the sacraments?

Do I thank Jesus for His unfailing love—for always being there for me?

Art: In fifteen minutes, draw as many things as possible that you are thankful for.

CHAPTER TWENTY-FOUR

Hurricane at Nob

Branches crash to the ground. A roof caves in. Tiles blow onto the road. Women scream, and frightened men try to calm them down. Trees bend—some topple. Lamps flicker and go out. It's a terrible storm.

Jesus opens the door of the house where He is staying with His apostles, and goes out. "Come back in!" Thaddeus shouts from the doorway, "You'll be killed."

Jesus stretches out His hand and prays. Then he commands, "That's enough! I want it!"

He goes back into the house. The wind gives one last howl and dies down. The huge silence then is in its own way deafening.

"What happened?" people ask. "How did it stop so suddenly?"

It begins to rain softly. The dust settles. The women yell, "The Lord! The Lord! He worked a miracle! Hosanna! Praise Jesus!" The women all keep shouting and praising.

People flock to the house where Jesus is; they all want

to touch Him, to kiss Him, to thank Him. Jesus would like them to go home, but He is very patient with them.

* * * * *

Do I thank God for His miracles?

Am I aware that God can do everything, that nothing is too hard for Him?

Do I thank God for good weather and good crops?

Am I patient with people who are very emotional? Jesus was.

Do I take time to think how Jesus would act in any given situation and try to behave likewise?

Art: Divide a paper into six parts. Draw six different pictures of water. Leave room under each one to write a small Thank You—for instance, Thank You, God, for rivers to fish in. Thank You, God, for lakes to water-ski on. Thank You, God, for a cold glass of water to drink.

CHAPTER TWENTY-FIVE

Jesus and the Samaritan Shepherd

Jesus and His apostles are hurrying along a road in Samaria when a shepherd boy and a shepherd with a big flock of sheep approach.

The shepherd is sad. He tells Jesus, "I had a beautiful wife. A Roman soldier wanted her and took her away. Now I am alone. My son, Reuben, fell on the mountain and slid down one side. Now his back is broken. The doctors can't fix it. They say he'll die soon. And this, after my only daughter died as a little girl."

Jesus asks kindly, "Who, then, is that boy tending your sheep?"

"That's my neighbor's child. He has eight brothers and sisters. The Romans took his father as a galley slave because he failed to see a drunk Roman on the road and ran over him. His father has since died."

"How do you know?"

"A fellow on the galley ship said he saw them dump his body into the sea. You don't last even three years on those

slave ships. I'm taking care of this boy because his mother can't take care of all of them. Another neighbor has three of the girls and the mother has four at home."

Jesus asks, "If Reuben were healed, would you still take care of this boy?"

Eagerly, the man nods. "Yes—he's like my son. And I believe that the rabbi in Palestine who is the Son of God could heal my son, if only I could find Him."

"You are speaking to Him," Jesus tells him.

The Samaritan is incredulous. "*You* are Jesus?"

"Yes, I am!" Jesus confirms.

"Please heal my son—I know You can!"

"It is done as you asked! Your faith has healed him," Jesus says to him.

The Samaritan falls to his knees and cries: "Thank you! I believe!" Then he rushes home. There he jumps for joy, dancing with his son.

* * * * *

Examine your conscience: are you thankful for all the good things that happen to you?

Do you take time to count your blessings? Are you really grateful for all the members of your family?

Think how terrible it would be if your parents disappeared. Think how lonely it would be if no one was left at home except you.

Right now, take time to thank God for each member of your family...even the ones who bug you and the ones you fight with.

CHAPTER TWENTY-SIX

Blind Man at Bethsaida

Peter leads a blind man by the hand to Jesus and says, "I'm bringing him to You, Jesus. He has been waiting to be healed." The blind man and several others implore, "Jesus, son of David, have mercy on us! Touch us and we will see. We believe in You."

Jesus takes the blind man by the hand and guides him away from the hot, bright sunshine of the street. He places him by a cool wall in the shade. Then He puts His hands gently against the man's closed eyes and prays. Jesus takes His hand away and asks, "What do you see?"

"I see what I think are some men passing by, but they are blurred. They must be men, because the shapes are walking." Jesus puts His hands on the man's eyes and prays some more. "*Now* what do you see?" He wants to know.

"I see the difference between the trees, the ground, and the men walking. And I see You! How handsome You are! Your eyes are so kind. Your

hair looks like sunbeams. Your smile comes from heaven. How beautiful You are! I adore You!" the man exclaims. He kneels down and kisses the hem of Jesus' tunic.

Jesus says, "Stand up and come to your mother, who has been your light and comfort since you were born—whose love you only know." Jesus takes the man by the hand and leads him to his mother, who has knelt down and is adoring Jesus.

"Stand up, woman, and take your son. He now sees daylight. May his heart follow the eternal light. May you go home and live in holiness for God. Do not tell anyone I cured you, because I need to get to another town and tell the people about the miracle." And Jesus disappears quickly along the path by the kitchen garden.

* * * * *

Now go to your secret place with Jesus and ask yourself these questions:

Do I appreciate my own health?

Do I thank God for eyes that see, and ears that hear, for legs that walk, and hands that work?

Do I thank God for my parents, teachers friends—all those who help me? Am I grateful for all the gifts of mind and heart that God has given me?

Activities: Listen to or sing these songs: "The Dawn Has Come," by Gregory Norbet, O.S.B.; Weston Priory, Listen album; "Praise the Lord, My Soul," by John Foley, S.J. St Louis Jesuits, Earthen Vessels.

Learn the song: "Open My Eyes," text and music by Jesse Manibuson, OCP all rights reserved.

Art: Divide a paper into three equal parts. Draw one gift God has given you in each section—for instance, you might have a talent for babysitting, for riding your bike, for helping at church, for math, for listening, for gardening, for making cookies, for baseball, for art.... Then, on the back of the paper, write a Thank You to God for these gifts.

Drama: Choose someone you trust to blindfold you and lead you around the classroom. How does it feel to be blind? How do you think the man at Bethsaida felt?

Do you know anyone who is partially or totally blind? If you do, write that person a friendly letter. Someone will read the letter to that person, and his or her day will be happier because of you.

CHAPTER TWENTY-SEVEN

Oh, What a Gift

Jesus and some of His apostles enter a poor, run-down village. They go to the end of a row of houses and open the rusty gate to Solomon's house. No one has lived in it for quite awhile, and it is quite dilapidated. Rats scurry in the storeroom. Weeds choke the garden.

While a small group are cleaning this mess up, three other apostles have found a poor old man, practically blind, trying to find wild chickory to eat. They bring him to Jesus and tell his story: "Master, this is Ananias. His son died, and his daughter-in-law threw him out. She didn't want to be bothered with an old man."

The old man says, "Where is the Master?"

"Over there. Can you see that long whiteness? That's his clothes," Peter tells him. Jesus comes forward and takes Ananias by the hand. "Are you all by yourself and you cannot see?"

"Yes, I'm all alone and I cannot see much at all. When I could see, I made baskets to sell and fixed fishnets. Now

I can't do that, so I beg and sleep under bridges. Lately, no one wants to feed me. I've been eating roots, but I can't see well enough to eat the good ones, so my stomach aches. If only my daughter-in-law had let me stay near my grandchildren…" his voice breaks. Jesus holds the old man and lets him weep. Then He asks Ananias, "Do you still own a house?"

"No, she sold it and took all the money, and told me to get out," the old man says.

"How do you live?" Jesus wants to know.

Ananias replies, "Like an animal."

Jesus asks, "Would you be willing to stay with Me and help Me?"

"Yes. Yes!" Ananias cries.

"All right, that is what we will do. You stay here and take care of this house that Solomon gave me. And you tend the yard. Then when we come here, we will have a place to stay. Do you like that idea?"

"Yes, but I am blind. I could learn the house, but I can't see well enough to tend a garden…."

Jesus bends over and kisses the man on his eyes.

"I can see! Oh, how wonderful!" The man is so happy he would fall over if Jesus wasn't supporting him.

"What joy does!" Peter exclaims in a husky voice, and a tear rolls down his cheek. Thomas says, "Ananias is hungry. Let's get him some food."

Ananias is so happy he wants to kiss the feet of Jesus.

"No, Father," Jesus says. "We'll go inside and get you some food and a new tunic, and then you will be among sons. Next, we'll fix the garden and get you some doves, so you'll have some living things for companionship. Then you can tell people about the Messiah."

"I will do that!" the old man exclaims. Jesus goes into the house, holding the old man by the hand. Peter wipes tears from his cheeks.

Andrew asks, "Why are you weeping, brother?"

"Mind your own business. His kindness moves me deeply. More so than when He thunders."

"But when He thunders, we see Him as King," Judas replies.

"But now we see the saint in Him," Peter replies. Then they start arguing whether Israel needs a king or a saint. The old man comes out, carrying a water jug, and they ask him: "What does Israel need to become great—a king or a saint?"

"It needs God, my sons. It needs that God in there praying. Be very good! What a gift—oh, what a gift God has given you in Him!" He waves his water jug and continues singing, "Oh, what a gift... what a wonderful gift."

* * * * *

Pause and consider in your quiet place:

Do I stop to consider all the gifts God has given to me—the happy gifts, like my parents, friends, good clothes, food, toys, the Mass, the Eucharist? The hard gifts, like work and obedience?

Do I take time to thank God for everything that happens to me?

Do I see everything God has made, either directly or indirectly, as a gift—roses, grass, ferns, trees, fields, tractors, streets, cars, cities, buildings, combines, plows, trucks, gardens, markets, freeways?

Yes, all that exists comes from God. Let us be thankful and say with Ananias, "Oh, what a gift!"

Songs: "On Eagles' Wings" by Michael Joncas, 1979 New Dawn Music OCP (Ps 91); "God's Greatest Gift" by Owen Alstott, 1995, 1999, OCP.

CHAPTER TWENTY-EIGHT

Marjiam's Grandfather Dies

Jesus is taking Marjiam to see his dear grandfather, Simon. Marjiam has been saving money in order to free him from bondage to a cruel Pharisee who beats his grandfather when he's too sick to work.

Marjiam has saved some honey, cheese, and olives to bring to Simon, along with two light summer tunics made by his adoptive mother. "If you love me," Marjiam had said to her, "make them for my grandfather." Peter and Porphira plan to have Simon stay with them once he has been released.

Jesus and Marjiam arrive, and the steward says, "Come quickly; he's very sick."

"Oh, Lord," Marjiam moans, and with Jesus, he runs into his grandfather's room. The old man is very pale and appears to be dying. He lies there motionless.

"Grandpa! Grandpa! I am Marjiam—do you understand? I'm your grandson." No response. Marjiam turns to Jesus. "Cure him—please!—so he can speak to me."

Jesus lays a hand on Simon's head. "Son of My Father, listen to Me." The old man opens his glassy eyes and tries unsuccessfully to speak.

"Grandpa, I have come," Marjiam says urgently. "I prayed so hard that I might come. Soon, I'll have enough money to get you out of here. You can live with us."

Simon finally manages to whisper, "May God reward you... but it's too late. I'm going to Abraham, to suffer no more." His eyes focus on Jesus. "Is it not so?"

"It is. Be in peace. I absolve you, Simon, from all your faults, and from sins that you may have committed. I forgive you. Go in peace."

Marjiam is weeping. Simon smiles and says, "One falls asleep peacefully with Your help, Jesus."

"Grandpa! Oh, he is dying. Let us give him some honey. His tongue is dry. He is cold. Honey warms one," Marjiam cries, searching in his bag with one hand and holding his grandfather's head steady with the other.

"I will hold him," Jesus says. "You get the honey." Marjiam pulls out a small jar and sticks his finger in. He puts some on Simon's lips, and his grandfather says, "It's good."

Then his grandfather puts his hand on Marjiam's brown hair and says, "You are good... better than honey. But your honey can't help anymore. Neither can your cool tunic. You keep them, with my blessing." Marjiam weeps and rests his head on the bed. The steward comforts him and says, "You are not alone. We love you. Jesus loves you." Then the old grandfather says, "I am happy."

Jesus embraces the old man and intones psalms 120 and 121. At the end of the fourth verse, He stops and says quietly, "Go in peace." The old man is dead. Marjiam doesn't notice. Jesus embraces Marjiam. "He is in peace, Marjiam.

This is the greatest gift a man can have, peace in God. You are not alone. We love you."

Marjiam says, "Thank You, Jesus, but I can't even give him a sepulchre."

The steward steps up, "Some disciples here will help us. I'll go arrange it."

Peter says, "But the Pharisee?"

"Don't worry. I'll tell him there's a dead man in here, and he won't come near for fear of being contaminated." They arrange a funeral with full honors for Marjiam's dear grandfather.

* * * * *

Examine your conscience by asking yourself:

Do I stop and think how important it is to live well so I can die well and be with God?

Am I willing to make sacrifices, like Marjiam, to help others?

Do I see daily prayer as important?

Am I light for others? Do I bring the message of Jesus to them?

Songs: "Hold Me in Life," (Ps 25) by Bernard Huijbers, or "Peace is Flowing Like a River" by Carey Landry.

CHAPTER TWENTY-NINE

Tamar and Fara

A man from Petra elbows his way through a big crowd surrounding Jesus. He is carrying a little girl with bandaged eyes, while a servant follows him carrying a blind boy with bandaged eyes.

People open up to let this group pass. The man and his servant lay the blind children before Jesus. The man says sorrowfully, "These are my children, Master."

"You have much faith, man. What would you have done if you hadn't found Me?"

"I would have kept looking."

"What about your caravan and all your material possessions?"

"They are not important, compared to spiritual things."

"Man, you have great faith. Uncover the girl's face," Jesus says.

The man hesitates. "I keep it covered because the light terribly hurts her eyes."

"It will only be a few seconds of pain," Jesus assures him.

The little girl begins to weep loudly and covers her bandaged eyes with her hands. Her father explains, "She is acting like that because the doctors burned her to make her eyes well."

"Don't be afraid," says Jesus to the girl. "What is your name?" She is sobbing so loudly she can't answer.

"Her name is Tamar," her father replies on her behalf.

"Don't cry, Tamar," Jesus tells her. "I won't hurt you. Feel My hands; I have nothing in them. First, I will heal your brother, and he will tell you how it felt. Come here, child."

The servant places Fara on Jesus' lap.

"Do you know who I am?" Jesus asks.

"You are Jesus of Nazareth, the Son of God and the rabbi of Galilee," Fara responds.

Jesus inquires, "Do you believe in Me?" and Fara nods.

Jesus lays His hands on the boy's eyes and says, "Be cured. May the light of your eyes open the way for the light of faith!" Jesus moves His hands away.

Fara lets out a shout. "Father, I can see!' Then he kisses Jesus on the cheek and gives Him a hug. Fara rests his head on Jesus' shoulder and snuggles up. His father wants to remove him, but Jesus reassures his father, "It's all right. Let him be. Now, Fara, tell your little sister how it felt."

"Tamar, it was gentle, like Mommy's hands. Come, be cured, so we can play together again."

Tamar reluctantly agrees.

The mean Pharisees start howling, "It's a trick. She's not blind. She's just pretending!"

Jesus very gently removes the bandages. There, for everyone to see, are two red, scabby sores out of which pus and tears are oozing. Horrible burns disfigure Tamar's eyebrows. The crowd gasps at the little girl's suffering.

Jesus puts His hands gently over her eyes and says, "Father, You gave light to Your children—give light to these eyes so she may see and believe in You." He removes His hands, and Tamar keeps her eyes closed.

"Open them, Tamar. Don't be afraid. It won't hurt you."

She slowly opens two big, dark eyes. "Father, I can see you!" Then she slowly relaxes on Jesus' shoulder.

The crowds rejoice and praise God. Tamar's father thanks Jesus and throws himself at Jesus' feet.

Jesus replies, "Your faith has been rewarded; may it lead you to God."

Tamar and Fara hug Jesus and say a last farewell before their father has his servants present rich gifts. Then they are off.

* * * * *

Ask yourself:

How much faith do I have?

Do I believe in Jesus?

Do I pray for what I need?

Do I take time to thank those who help me, especially parents and grandparents?

Am I more interested in spiritual things than material things?

Learn the song: "Now Thank We All Our God," Johann Crüger, 1598–1662, Felix Mendelssohn, 1809–1847.

CHAPTER THIRTY

Longinus

A handsome soldier, Longinus, is patrolling a street in Jerusalem. He is riding a beautiful white horse, freshly shod so that the new shoes make a metal click against the cobblestones as he canters down the street. Longinus' metal helmet gleams in the sun.

Suddenly a little Jewish child no more than two years old toddles out into the street. The Roman reins in quickly, but he can't stop in time. The horse's hoof hits the boy's head and fractures his skull. Blood gushes out of a terrible wound. Longinus leaps off his horse and picks up the child, whose mother comes running out screaming. She grabs her dying son away from the soldier.

Longinus mutters, "I need Jesus," and he rushes into the Temple. The Pharisees see him enter and they hiss, "Roman pig! Get out!"

"Let me alone!" he snaps angrily and goes straight for Jesus, who quickly accompanies Longinus out before the Pharisees take action in addition to their vile words.

Jesus approaches the mother holding her dying child. She is so upset she can't hear Jesus trying to console her. Finally, Jesus reaches over and says, "Give Me your child." She does so in a daze.

The rag around the little one's head is soaked with blood. Jesus holds the child close, kisses his forehead, and says, "Be healed." The little boy's fingers turn rosy, and he begins to breathe again.

Then Jesus turns to the Roman soldier and says, "I need some water to wash away the blood." The soldier says, "I'll get some." He takes off his tin helmet, runs to the well, and comes back with a helmet full of water. Now the child is babbling happily as Jesus washes off the blood. There remains only a long scar on his head. The little boy pulls playfully on Jesus' beard as He hands him back to his mother.

"Thank You—thank You! I believe You are the Son of God!" she exclaims. The Roman soldier says, "I am so grateful that You came right away. I never want to hurt anyone, especially not a child. You are indeed the Messiah. Lord Jesus, I thank You."

"You are a good man, Longinus. Persevere in your good ways, and heaven will bless you." The Roman soldier salutes and goes back to his job. Jesus peacefully goes back to the Temple.

* * * * *

In your secret place, in the presence of Jesus, examine your conscience by asking yourself:

Am I kind to all people even those of different races?

When I am angry do I use vile language? Does this language hurt others?

If I cause a problem or an accident, do I get help immediately? Do I face my mistakes?

Do I run to Jesus?

Am I afraid of what people will think of me?

Do I accept my sins and my mistakes without getting discouraged?

Am I cheerful about trying again when I have failed?

Learn the song: "One Bread, One Body," by John Foley, S.J. OCP.

Activity: Act out this story and see if you can bring out the kindness and care of Jesus and Longinus.

CHAPTER THIRTY-ONE

Storm at Sea

Jesus asks a group of apostles—Peter, John, James, Thaddeus, Simon Zealot, and Matthew—to accompany a disciple, John of Endor, and a freed Greek slave to Antioch. A Cretan man, Nicomedes, runs the ship that will take them. A terrible storm arises before they get out of the Mediterranean. The ship shudders and flounders. It's as if all hell has broken loose.

Nicomedes, a Greek sailor, and Peter are the only ones on the deck. A piece of mast comes crashing down and strikes the sailor on the head. He falls on the deck, badly injured. The captain yells to Peter, "Get below deck! Go!"

"What about that man?" Peter shouts back.

"If he's not already dead, he will be."

"Give him to me," says Peter.

"Anything you like, but just get below the deck!" roars the captain.

Peter creeps up to the motionless man on the slippery deck and pulls him toward the hatch. Peter mumbles, "His

head is split like a ripe pomegranate. Jesus should be here."
He loads the dying man on his shoulders and is quickly
soaked with his blood.

The Cretan captain yells, "It's quite useless!"

Peter says, "We shall see." He opens the hatch and yells
down, "James, John—come help me." They come running,
and all three lower the wounded man to the berth below.

Peter says to a nearby woman, "Can you fix this?"

"Yes," she replies, "but I need plenty of water."

"Well, we are not short of water around here," someone
else says. and they bring her a tub full.

Syntyche applies wet compresses until she gets the
wound to stop bleeding. The sailor begins to come around.
He mumbles and gasps for breath. His eyes open and he
says, "Am I dying?"

"No," Syntyche replies, "you're going to be all right.
You will recover. Lie still and rest." She takes his hand and
talks to him in Greek. He relaxes at hearing his own
familiar language. Next, she applies some ointment that the
Blessed Mother gave her. She asks the apostles to pray for
the injured Greek, and they all pray.

She bandages the sailor's head snugly with strips of
clean cloth. The bleeding stops. He dozes off to sleep.

The hatch flies open.

"What's the matter?" asks Peter.

"We're in great danger. We're likely to capsize. The captain wants incense to offer to the goddess Venus," the sailor
explains. "We're in her sea."

"Forget such nonsense!" Peter replies.

"I have to get it, or he'll throw me overboard," the
frantic sailor replies. He grabs the incense and rushes back
on deck. The captain finally lights the incense and throws

the offering overboard. The storm worsens. Peter, James, and John watch from the deck.

"Get below!" the captain shouts, adding, "We need a miracle."

"Let us pray and you will get your miracle," Peter says to him.

"All right—anything!" cries the frantic captain.

"Sing, John," says Peter, and John sings to Mary.

Then they pray the prayer Jesus taught them not so long ago to Our Father. The captain watches scornfully. They sing and pray some more. The waves calm down.

The expression on the captain's face is incredulous. He can hardly believe his own eyes. Peter casts a sidelong glance at him, but keeps on praying. Finally, the sea is very quiet. No waves crash over the deck anymore.

"Well, what did you do? What formula is it?" asks the pagan captain.

"That of the true God and his handmaid," replies Peter.

"Give me your formula; I'm willing to pay for it!" bargains the captain.

"Sacred things can't be bought. You have to believe in the true God," Peter gently explains.

* * * * *

Examine your conscience by asking yourself:

Do I show respect for what is sacred?

Do I take holy things for granted?

Do I take time to realize the power of the Eucharist?

Do I pray when I'm in trouble?

Do I realize that singing is a way of praying?

Do I realize that every part of the Mass has a special

meaning, and that God will work miracles if we have faith and are open to them?

Song: "Star Above the Ocean, Maria," OCP 1997, text, Sister Jeanne Frolick, SFCC; Music: Munster 1855. Listen to the song and sing it. Then write a prayer asking Mary to give you more faith in Jesus. Thank Jesus for the gift of His Mother.

CHAPTER THIRTY-TWO

Patience

You wiggle in your school seat and wish the day was over. Your dad promised to take you and your brother on a hiking, camp-out fishing trip this weekend.

Your teacher is taking up a quiz about verbs. Whoever invented verbs, anyway? What a dull subject! How many fish did a verb ever catch? Just then, your teacher asks you: "Is question number seven a linking verb or an action verb?"

"What's the difference?" you ask innocently. She gives you a withering look and calls on Joe. *Sure, sure*, you think to yourself, *that walking encyclopedia always knows*. He answers expertly, and you give him your best hate-look.

Verbs go on for another ten minutes, which seems like a century. Finally, the last prayer is said, and the buzzer sounds. You race down the hall, get nabbed by the principal, and have to go back and walk.

Your dad is waiting in the car. He smiles as you climb in and dump your book bag. Your brother is already there. Your

mom opted to stay home, but has packed all the food and gear. You are finally there. You smell the pines and look at the big lake. You help set up the tent and gather firewood.

The next morning, the sun is barely peeking out when you head for the lake. An hour passes—no bites. Your brother lands a lovely trout. You get nothing.

"This is almost as bad as verbs!" you mutter. Your dad laughs and replies, "Rome wasn't built in one day."

"Who cares about Rome?" you remark.

He laughs again. "Be patient. There's a lot of trout down there." Another hour; no fish. "Rat Spit!" you say, jumping up and heading for the tent, "I'm going hiking. This stuff is too slow."

"All right," calls your dad, "but stay on the upper trail."

You take off. The trail is hot, dry, and dusty. There are hikers. You meet Jesus. He invites you to sit under a huge fir tree in the cool shade.

You begin: "It's awful. Everything is so slow. School is slow. The fish don't bite. I am sick and tired of waiting! What good is there in waiting?"

"The best things in life come slowly," Jesus says. "When you plant a little seed, it takes time for it to grow. When an idea starts in your brain, you have to give it time to develop. Worthwhile things always take time. Things that are forced, like Easter lilies, take a whole year to gain back their strength. Athletes that force their muscles by steroids ruin their bodies for life. It's important to take time, to allow things to grow at their right speed. Why are you so impatient?"

"I dunno," you reply. "I just like things to move, and I feel upset when they don't. It seems *dumb* to be always waiting. Can you tell me anything good that comes from waiting?"

"Yes—the whole world waited for thousands of years

for the Messiah, and since He came, the world has not been the same. It has changed for the better. People think about others. People care. People love. Sit still and think about waiting. Remember how the Prophet Isaiah said: 'But they that wait on the LORD Shall renew their strength...'." (Isaiah 40:31.)

"Well... okay, Lord, give me patience right away."

Jesus laughs and you look puzzled. "What's so funny?" you ask, somewhat indignantly. "You are," He says, and He slips away.

* * * * *

You lean your head against the giant fir tree and begin to think about patience:

Patience... the ability to let things happen.

Patience... the ability not to pull up the plant to see if the roots are growing.

Patience... the ability to let God be God in your life.

Patience... not pushing or wanting more than God gives you at the moment.

Music: "They That Wait Upon the Lord."

CHAPTER THIRTY-THREE

Rain Forest

You find yourself on the edge of a great rain forest in Brazil. The strange part is that you are not your-self—you are a monkey.

You swing from tree to tree. It's fun. It's exhilarating. Tropical birds hang above you. Their bright red and yellow markings contrast with the dense green jungle. Huge snakes with long, sticky tongues crawl beneath you. It's quite an adventure. You pause in your swinging to eat coconuts and bananas.

Then you curl up in a tree and go to sleep. The shrill cry of a bird awakens you, and you open your eyes just in time to see a huge snake slithering up the tree toward you. Quickly, you scamper to another tree. You swing among small branches where the snake can't go. Safe, you hear your friends chattering behind you.

Next, you climb to the top of a large tree, where you watch the jungle trail. Two men are approaching, carrying machetes. You hear them talk. They are planning to build a

road through the jungle. You envy them. They can do what they want, and you can't. You have to do monkey things all your life—how very boring.

You turn to your monkey friend and exclaim, "Free will—wouldn't you like to have free will?"

"No, I wouldn't," he replies, "With free will, I would be responsible for all my actions. I don't want to be responsible. I'd rather be a monkey and follow my instincts."

"Well, *I* wouldn't," you retort. "I'd rather decide what I'm going to do." Then you leave the jungle and slip off to your secret place. You sit very still and think:

Free will? What does 'free will' mean? Would I prefer to be a monkey and never have to decide? How free am I? Freedom is the right to do as I ought... not the license to do what I please or feel like. I am never free to hurt anyone else or to infringe on someone else's rights.

Freedom is sharing the goodness of God. Can I use my freedom for what it truly is? Jesus said: "You shall know the truth, and the truth will make you free." What *is* truth? How free am I? How do God's laws make me free?

The teacher told us in religion today that the more we keep God's laws, the more free we are. She said when we are free from sin, we are really free.

I just don't understand... but maybe someday I will.

* * * * *

Learn the song: "It's a Long Road to Freedom," Maryknoll Missionary Sisters.

Art: Draw symbols of people who were free in God, who did God's will. For example, in the Old Testament:
Abraham—altar of sacrifice;

Moses—staff stretched over Red Sea;
New Testament:
Mary—Yes to God!
Joseph—staff or lily with "yes" on it.

CHAPTER THIRTY-FOUR

Who is Jesus to Me?

J esus said: "And you, who do you say that I am?"
Peter replied, "You are Christ, the Son of the Living
God."

Jesus walks along with you on the beach and sits down
on a log. He motions you to sit down. You put your football on the sand under one bare toe and sit down.

Jesus says, "And you? Who do *you* say that I am? Am I
a football player? Am I an itinerant preacher? Am I a car-
penter? Am I the son of Mary?

You wiggle your toes in the sand and reflect: *Who is
Jesus to me?*

Jesus continues: "Am I your God? Am I your white
Host? Am I your friend? Am I your helper? Am I a miracle
worker—a magician to bring people back to life, putting
sight in blind eyes? Am I a fixer-upper? Am I a basketball
star? Who am I to you?

"Stop! Think! Be still and see for yourself that 'I am the
LORD your God.' (Psalm 46:11)

"Where am I in your life? Can you talk to Me? Are you comfortable in My presence? What do you like best about Me? Do you like My expressive eyes? Do you like My kindness? How well do you know Me?

"Come, let us go to your secret place and think about these questions."

* * * * *

Art: Draw the 'many hats' of Jesus: football, baseball, soccer, bike helmet, snow hat, straw hat, etc. Write a one-line prayer with each hat.

Learn the song: "Lord, You Have Come," by Cesareo Gabarain.

CHAPTER THIRTY-FIVE

Mission

Jesus is thirty years old, and preparing to set out on His mission. It has been a year since St. Joseph died. Mary fixes a lovely dinner with baked fish, freshly baked, big round brown loaves, and fresh garden vegetables. Jesus doesn't feel like eating, but He eats just to please His Mother. Mary is sad and trying not to cry.

Finally, the meal is over, and Jesus gets up to go. Mary has already packed His knapsack with clean clothes, cheese, bread, olives and apples. Tears glisten in Mary's eyes as she kisses Him goodbye.

"Remember, Mother, I must fulfill the mission My Father gave Me," Jesus tells her gently.

"I understand, Son—I want You to do Our Father's will, but I will miss You."

"And I'll miss You, too."

Jesus holds His Mother in His arms for a last farewell, and then He goes down the road. Mary stands in the door and watches until a bend in the road hides Jesus from view.

Mary goes back into the house, washes up the dishes, and puts the food away. "Yahweh," Mary says, "please give my son a safe, warm place to sleep tonight...."

When she has finished straightening up the kitchen, Mary then goes into her small bedroom and prays. She crouches down and sits on her heels, as is the Jewish custom.

Jesus continues down the road. He walks several days and comes to a large lake, where two strong fishermen are casting in their nets. He beckons: "Come, follow Me." The younger one, Andrew, throws down the net and runs after Jesus. The older one, Peter, listens to Jesus while doing what has to be done to take care of the nets and boat.

"Who are you?" Andrew asks.

"I am the Messiah, come and see," Jesus replies.

"What is your mission?" Andrew questions.

"I have been sent to catch men, just the way you catch fish... with the net of truth. Come and see."

"I will come. I want to know more," Andrew replies. And by now, Peter is ready to go with Jesus, too.

* * * * *

Jesus speaks to you in your secret place: "Follow Me. Follow Me, today. Come to Me with all your heart. Come and I will show you what I want you to do today. I have a mission for you."

You look startled: "What is my mission? Where am I to be sent? What must I do? How can I be sure You are sending me, Lord? Am I supposed to help someone? How? A word? A smile? A friendly gesture?

"How, Lord? Tell me, for I do want to follow You."

CHAPTER THIRTY-SIX

Galley Slaves

Jesus heads for a Roman-occupied town, and Peter objects: "Who can You speak to there? Who will listen to You—the waves?"

"The waves were created by God, too. I want to speak near the galley ships." The apostles stand around with glum faces, because they don't like the Romans.

Jesus begins speaking and says, "The man who thinks he needs no one, not even God, is foolish. A man proves his worth by deeds, not by words."

A street vendor listens. Then a high-ranking Roman comes by and asks, "Hail, Master—do you know me?"

"May God come to you, Publius," Jesus replies.

"I'm happy You came to the Roman sector. I was hoping to see You again," Publius tells Him.

Jesus asks him, "Are there many men chained to the oars on that galley ship?"

"Yes, quite a number, mostly war prisoners. Are You interested in them?"

"Yes, I would like to approach their ship."

"I'll take you out." The Roman takes Jesus to the big ship in a little boat. Jesus speaks to the slaves and tells them about their souls, which will never die. He tells them that God loves them, and that He is their brother who will give His life for the ransom of their souls. By this time, a great number of Romans have gathered and are listening.

Jesus says, "If man used his brains, he would never commit a crime." Publius likes that, and responds, "By Jove! Wonderful words! I must remember them. You are truly a great man."

Jesus replies, "Everyone who wants to be could be as faithful as I am if he were one with God."

"By Jove! That makes sense!" Publius replies.

Then Jesus asks, "Could I give some comfort, some help to those poor galley slaves, so that they'll know I love them? I have some money for fruit and wine."

"Give it to me. I can do that. But there is a prominent lady in that golden litter over there who can do much more. I will ask her." Publius goes to the gold-and-silk litter, and speaks through the curtains.

Then Publius comes back to Jesus. "Yes, Claudia has given me much for the slaves. I will distribute it, so that the jailers don't gobble it up first."

While Publius distributes food to the galley slaves, Jesus explains to Claudia what her soul is. He says, "You are famous because you belong to the Claudi family. A person is even more so because he belongs to God."

Publius comes back, happy, and says, "That will be the first time a Roman soldier dealt mercifully with war slaves." Jesus smiles at him and goes His way.

* * * * *

Jesus invites you to sit quietly in your secret place and think about this story.

Can you remember that he came for all?

Can you remember Jesus wants you to be a messenger of hope to today's galley slaves—the downtrodden, the pushed aside, the child that no one wants to sit by?

Do you secretly put down a child who has trouble learning or who has miserable manners in the lunchroom? Do you refuse to play with such children or talk to them?

Do you look down on someone who doesn't have nice clothes or belongings?

Stop, think, act today to bring hope to someone who feels hopeless.

Listen to this song: "Comfort My People," by Sister Marianne Misetich, and then make a poster of two ways in which today you are going to bring hope and comfort to someone. It could be outside of school. You can keep this secret.

CHAPTER THIRTY-SEVEN

Using the Hard Stuff

Joe is watching his grandmother make cookies. He's feeling rather down because he didn't make the soccer team.

He tells her, "Grandma, I tried so hard. I worked a *lot* harder than the new kid who got in."

"Here, have a taste of this—it will make you feel better," and Grandma offers him a spoonful of flour.

"Yuck! Who likes flour?" Joe explodes angrily, refusing.

"Then, how about a bit of raw egg?"

"Grandma, what's wrong with you? You *know* I don't like raw eggs!" Joe exclaims.

"I understand, Joe. I'm just trying to help you see that these hard things in your life—last week your bike was stolen, this week you didn't make the team—are one way God helps us to grow.

"I'm not saying it's God's fault, or that God did it on purpose. I'm just saying that everything works together for good if we let it. If you put together these things that individually

116

aren't good to eat, like flour and eggs and sugar, they can make something good."

"How?" Joe asks skeptically.

"Well, all right. You like cookies, right?" his grandmother points out.

Not sure where she is taking this, Joe agrees: "Sure, who doesn't?"

"But you don't like the separate ingredients. You like to have a strong character, a disciplined character, but it takes training. Perhaps these setbacks are training—maybe you could use them to be a better person."

"How can any of these things make me a better person?" Joe ponders.

"You'll be more sympathetic with Willie, who didn't make the team last year *or* this year. And, remembering how horrible it is to have your bike stolen, you'll work at being very honest even in tiny ways," his grandmother says to him.

She pulls out a tin of freshly baked cookies. "Have a cookie and remember how bad-tasting ingredients come together into something good."

* * * * *

Can you trust God to blend all the "bad stuff" into something good?

Can you remember to go to God when things are falling apart?

Do you really believe that all things work together for good for those who love God?

Song: "God's Circle of Love," Carey Landry.

CHAPTER THIRTY-EIGHT

Hillside Message

You are walking through a time tunnel, going back, back, back, to A.D. 31. The Apostle John is your guide. "Come," he says, "Let's join the rest of them."

You find yourself on a beautiful, grassy hillside, with some 5,000 people of all ages. It is springtime: large daisies and little pink-and-blue flowers cover the hillside. A little girl, about five years old, and her older playmate are picking flowers. You watch what they do—they squeeze through the vast crowd and go right to Jesus.

The five-year-old hugs Jesus and starts sticking flowers in His belt. Her older companion shakes her head—"Don't do that," she reprimands the little one, who replies, "I want Jesus to look nice."

"You're bugging Him," her friend says.

"No," Jesus tells the children, "she's not bugging Me. I like flowers. Let her alone." Smiling, the smaller girl continues decorating Him. Jesus pats her shoulders and thanks her. Satisfied, she sits down. Her companion looks on. You sit down, too, and Jesus begins teaching the eight

Beatitudes. The people listen.

You can't keep your eyes off Him. His face is kind. His dark hair shines in the warm sunshine and His beard has a bit of reddish blonde in it. His eyes are thoughtful. The people listen all morning with only a few short breaks—even the small children are not fussy. All of a sudden, it's noon, and the people are hungry.

Peter and John look worried. "What will we do, Master? How can we feed all these people?" they wonder. "We have only one boy with five loaves and two fish."

Jesus smiles and says, "Have all the people sit down."

The twelve apostles scatter through the crowd and get everyone seated.

Then Jesus says, "Now bring Me the boy with the five loaves and two fish." Andrew calls him over. He smiles and hands to Jesus his loaves and fish. Jesus points to twelve empty baskets from yesterday's lunch. "Bring Me those," He directs. They do.

He places a small piece of bread and a tiny morsel of dried fish in each basket. "Now, go feed the hungry." You watch as the twelve-year-old boy picks up his basket. The pieces of bread and fish grow right before your eyes! You look at the other baskets. It happens, again and again, until everyone is fed.

The people are smiling and happy. Even Judas, who at first wouldn't believe, now does. You watch in wonder, and then go to your secret place.

You sit very still, and pray: "Bread of heaven, feed me and help me never to put down a little girl with flowers. Make me gentle and strong." True gentleness is very strong.

* * * * *

M u s i c : Pan de Vida.

119

Mary's Flowers

You and a friend are hiking in a deep woods. Trilliums and sword ferns line your path. Birds twitter overhead in tall firs and low-spreading vine maples. You feel warm sunshine filter through the trees. It's a perfect day for hiking— no homework, no one yelling at you to clean your room, no one telling you to empty the dishwasher or feed the dog. Ah, yes, it's a perfect day— peace and the company of a friend!

After you two have hiked for three miles, you stop to rest. You sit on a fallen tree. You notice some small white flowers at your feet.

"Look, I've never seen these before!" you exclaim.

"I haven't, either," your friend says, bending over to see them more closely.

Just then, you hear twigs snap behind you, and a tall, handsome man steps out of the brush.

"Jesus! What are You doing here?" you exclaim.

"I want to tell you about those flowers," He says, and sits down.

120

"They are My Mother's favorite. They bloomed in My grandmother's garden before My Mother was born. St. Anne loved them, too," Jesus says, bending over and picking a small white flower. "See, they are called the Star of Bethlehem. When I was your age, I always brought these to My Mother every spring. She loves flowers." Jesus smiles and waves the flower in front of your nose. "Such a delicate fragrance. Do you want to hear about the flowers in My Mother's life?"

"Yes we'd like that," you say.

When the Angel Gabriel came to tell Mary she was to be the Mother of God, Mary had a big vase of pink almond blossoms in her room. The dazzling angel in white looked beautiful by those fresh pink blossoms. Flowers played an important part in her life. Jesus continues: "And after I died on the cross, My Mother came back later with John to Calvary. There, at the spot where My cross stood, was a red flower blooming. It had green leaves in the shape of a heart. Mother carefully dug up the little flower and took it home." Here, Jesus stops and picks one more flower. He gives us each one.

"Do you know what tomorrow is?" He asks.

"No, what?" you respond.

"May first—it's the month of My Mother. Don't be afraid to bring a flower to My Mother every day of her month!"

Then He turns to your friend and says: "And you, young man, when you get a little older—don't hesitate to bring a flower to the girl you care about. There is no better way to show respect and love."

Your friend's jaw drops open, and he smiles because he does have a friend.

Then Jesus disappears and you are left sitting there with

a Star of Bethlehem in your hand. Your friend says: "I'll race you back to our secret place."

"Deal!"

You race. Winded, you stop. You each go into your secret place. You sit down and talk to Mary, your Heavenly Mother: "I want to be like your Son. I want to be the very best person I can be. Tomorrow I'll bring you a flower, I promise."

* * * * *

Music: "Sing of Mary," text: Roland F. Palmer, b.1891; Music: Christian Lyre, 1830.

CHAPTER FORTY

Journey of Love

The distance between Nazareth and Bethlehem is about eighty miles. Joseph walked, and Mary rode on the poor little donkey with the droopy brown ears and a little, frazzled tail. The wind was so icy, Joseph insisted on wrapping his big brown cloak around Mary.

When they finally got to the one inn in Bethlehem, Joseph tried to bribe a young man to give him his room by paying him double: "My wife is expecting a baby any minute, and we need privacy!"

The rude man laughed and said, "Tough! I'm not giving up my room." Joseph was sad and hurt.

Next, he begged the innkeeper, who said: "I have no rooms to spare, not even an empty hall!"

A young shepherd came running up. "Sir, there are some caves about a mile from here where you can find shelter." Joseph led the donkey to the caves. It was getting dark. A cold wind was still blowing. The first cave they came to was hewn out of rock and had a wooden beam supporting the center section.

He tended the fire nervously, expecting the birth of Jesus any minute. He carefully hung his brown cloak over the doorway to keep out the wind and make it more private.

Suddenly, a bluish-white light startled Joseph and made the whole cave as bright as noonday! He heard a baby's first cry. Joseph went over to where Mary was holding the Baby Jesus. Mary said, "Here, you hold Him while I unpack His clothes."

Joseph was very nervous, because this was the Son of God, but when he saw how cold the baby was, he took Him and wrapped his tunic sleeves around Him, and held Him close to his heart.

Then Mary washed Him and dressed Him while Joseph fixed the manger bed by folding Mary's softest mantle to put under Him. Then they laid Jesus in the manger and adored him.

Meanwhile, out in the fields, the shepherds had hired a new boy, twelve-year-old Levi, just that day. Most of the shepherds were in the big sheep shelter, looking out. "What's wrong with that new boy?" they wondered among themselves. "He's gawking at the sky. Looks as if he's lost his mind."

"Wait a minute, Reuben. Let's go see what it is he's looking at."

The shepherds stepped out, looked at the sky, and gasped in astonishment. "Look at that! Angels!"

"Listen! What a message! Let's go see the new King!"

They walked quickly toward the cave. When they got there, the older shepherds felt nervous, so they shoved Levi in first. Mary put her arm around the twelve-year-old, who felt a little awkward. Then she smiled at the others peeking in and welcomed them.

Levi knelt down and kissed the baby's feet. Then the other shepherds got enough courage to come forward and worship. Jesus began to cry. One shepherd said, "The mother is so young she doesn't have milk yet. Here, I'll milk my ewe."

He got out his wooden bowl and milked his ewe. Then he showed Mary how to put a clean piece of linen cloth into the milk and let the baby suck on that. Jesus did, and his crying stopped. The shepherd smiled. Everyone was happy. When it was time to go, the shepherds backed out, leaving their hearts behind.

* * * * *

And I? Do I adore Jesus in my heart? In the Tabernacle? In other people?

Am I reverent and respectful of people? Do I honor God's presence in all people?

Am I willing to share, or do I act like the rude young man who was unwilling to bunk elsewhere and let Joseph have his room?

Now, take a little time to sit quietly with Jesus in your secret place and think about all the journeys of love that God might ask of you: to go to the store when you would rather play with your friends, or perhaps to take care of a younger child when you would rather ride your bike.

Think what answer you would give if you were asked to go on a journey of love. What if God asked you to be a priest or a sister, and go to Africa? Could you go on *that* journey of love?

Song: "Gloria," by Sister Marianne Misetich, SNJM; used with permission.

CHAPTER FORTY-ONE

The Resurrection

It is very early Sunday morning—there is just a little pink streak in the eastern sky. Two guards are lounging on the ground by the tomb. The sepulchre has been sealed with white lime and the big red wax seal of the Temple. There are some ashes and half-burned twigs on the ground where the guards have been trying to keep warm. There is also a bit of leftover food. Near the food are some clean, dry animal bones they used to play a gambling game. Their gambling board sits near the bones.

In the east, a ball of fire descends brighter than the sun. The white light comes zooming down faster than I can read this. There is a loud, harmonious rumble as the light hits the stone and rolls it away. The Spirit of Christ enters and His Body is recomposed. The astonished guards fall over flat on their faces. They peer at the light but stay down. Jesus emerges from the tomb, but they can't see Him.

* * * * *

Jesus is new life. He wants me to have new life, and to leave behind all the bad stuff of the past. Can I let go of any past hurtful thoughts? Can I let His new life enter into me? Sit still and think about this.

Songs: "I Am the Resurrection" by Jim Anderson, Oregon Catholic Press; "I Know My Redeemer Lives," by Duke Street, LM.

CHAPTER FORTY-TWO

Jesus Appears to His Mother

Mary is in a little room next to the supper room. She is stretched out on the floor, praying. She is sad. She has the veil of Veronica with Jesus' face on it. She knows Jesus will rise, but she is thinking about the terrible sufferings He has gone through, and her heart shudders. She hears the window-shutter banging. She looks up. There is Jesus, smiling. He is handsome, dressed in a white garment that looks as if it were woven out of light.

Mary exclaims, "My Lord and my God!"

Jesus says, "Mother!" There is joy, freedom, and love in that cry. He lifts her up and kisses her. Mary kisses His hands and feet and head—all His wounds. A bright light comes from each wound.

Jesus says, "Kiss My heart, Mother, for your kiss will take away My last sorrow. Mother, it is all over. Redemption has taken place. Thank you for conceiving Me, for raising Me, for loving Me."

* * * * *

Jesus asks you to sit still and to think how much He loves you. He loved you enough to give His life.

How much do *you* love?

Can you make little sacrifices?

Do you appreciate your mother?

Do you take time to tell your mother how grateful you are for all she does?

Do you do little jobs cheerfully?

Songs: "Mary," by Sister Marianne Misetich, SNJM; used with permission. "Mary's Song," by Millie Rieth, OCP; "Sing of Mary," OCP; text by Roland F. Palmer, music by Christian Lyre.

CHAPTER FORTY-THREE

Jesus Appears to Lazarus

Most of the apostles and disciples have gathered at Lazarus' beautiful house after the death of Jesus. They are sad and discouraged.

Maximus, Lazarus' servant, is trying to get them to eat a breakfast of milk, honey, and fresh bread. No one feels like eating. He coaxes them, and they nibble a little. Philip is sitting outside by the fountain with his head down, dejected and crying. He won't even come into the house. Lazarus calls, "Philip, come in! Let us love one another for His sake. Let us be united."

"I ran away. I'm no good. I can't come in."

"Can you forgive yourself?" Lazarus asks.

"I *can't* forgive myself."

"Jesus wants you to forgive yourself. He told me to tell all of you that He forgives you," Lazarus assures the disciples.

Philip finally comes into the house. Peter tries to console him. Lazarus speaks to all of them—he reminds them how much Jesus loves them. Then He looks out the door and

says, "I'm coming, Lord."

The apostles look at each other and say, "What has he seen? What has he heard?"

"Maybe he's not well. Perhaps he's seeing things."

Lazarus smiles and says again, "I'm coming, Lord." The apostles shake their heads.

Lazarus runs out into the garden and falls on his knees, "Oh, my Lord."

Jesus appears in light and says, "Tell the apostles to come to the supper room. I ask another sacrifice of you. Stay here and rescue My disciples. They are like scattered sheep. Keep growing greater in My love." Jesus touches his forehead and blesses Lazarus, and then disappears in light. Lazarus runs back and says, "He has risen. He wants you to go to Him. He loves you." The apostles are dumfounded.

* * * * *

Examine your conscience by asking yourself:

How trusting am I?

Do I really believe that Jesus forgives me?

Do I easily become discouraged when I have made a mistake or done something wrong? Am I willing to try again?

Do I say the Act of Hope often and really mean it?

Song: "How Can I Keep From Singing?" (Quaker Hymn), Oregon Catholic Press, PO Box 18030, Portland, OR 97218-0030 phone 503 2R1-1191.

CHAPTER FORTY-FOUR

Pentecost

You go back in a time-tunnel to A.D. 33 and the Upper Room in Jerusalem. Eleven apostles and the Blessed Mother are there. You have to pound hard on the door before they let you in, and it is Our Lady who opens the door for you. The apostles look frightened. They are seated, praying, in a big circle. Mary and John are the only ones who don't look afraid.

You ask St. Peter, "Why are you afraid?"

"Because Jesus was murdered," he responds, "and we'll probably be next."

"Really? Why would they murder you?"

"You don't know? Because we are His followers."

"Oh…" you say.

John says, kindly, "Why don't you sit down and pray with us?" You sit down, and there is the sound of a strong wind. The shutters outside bang. The lamp goes out. John closes the shutters and relights the lamp. The wind gets stronger and makes a whistling noise. You look around.

Everyone is praying. They all look panicky, except Mary and John. Suddenly, you see flames over each person's head. You feel nervous until you look at Mary. Peace radiates from her and you begin to be peaceful. You touch her shoulder lightly and whisper, "What's happening?"

"The Holy Spirit is descending on each one. Pray and receive wisdom and and peace."

You sit still and say, "Come, Holy Spirit—fill the hearts of the faithful. Come right now; with Your strength, Your wisdom, and Your love. Fill our hearts and fill the world. Thank you, Holy Spirit."

* * * * *

Song: "Come Holy Ghost," or any Holy Spirit song.

Art: Draw seven flames and put the seven gifts in each one. Write a short prayer under each one.

CHAPTER FORTY-FIVE

The Upper Room

There are many iron bars across the windows in the upper room where Mary and the apostles are sitting, and the door is double-locked. A tiny beam of sunlight shines through the barred windows and plays on the floor. Mary is reading aloud from Scripture, and the apostles are praying. Mary finishes the scroll and puts it down.

All of a sudden, there is a rumble like a mighty wind. The chandelier above tinkles, and a bright ball of fire appears. The fire makes a circle like a big wreath around the head of Mary, and rests on the foreheads of each apostle in the form of a single flame. It remains for a time, and then vanishes.

Great peace descends on the apostles, and everyone feels the joy of the Holy Spirit. John points to Mary and whispers, "She is the altar, and the glory of God has rested on her." Mary is praying and she is very happy.

Peter is very excited and cries out, "Let us go and preach the Lord."

* * * * *

Sit quietly and think:

How well do I know the Holy Spirit?

Do I pray to the Holy Spirit? Do I ask the Holy Spirit to guide me? Am I aware that the Holy Spirit will give me wisdom if I only ask?

Oh, Holy Spirit, Fire of Love, help me to be the best person I can be. Help me today to always look for the good in others.

Song: "Come Holy Spirit," by Sister Marianne Misetich, SNJM. Used with permission.

CHAPTER FORTY-SIX

Marjiam and Porphira

Peter and his wife, Porphira, have no children. Jesus has promised the orphan boy, Marjiam, to them. Peter is very happy and excited about this. They have just gotten off the boat and are walking up to Peter's house. Marjiam takes Peter's hand and says, "What if your wife doesn't want me?"

"She will! She loves children, and she couldn't have any of her own." Then Peter turns to Jesus and says, "Will you explain everything to Porphira?"

"I'd be happy to," Jesus smiles.

All three arrive at the kitchen door. Porphira greets them, "Master! Simon! Welcome! I'm happy to see you. Come in—you must be tired."

"We have a boy," Peter says.

"An orphan we found along the way," John explains.

"Oh, my! Come here!" she says, getting down to Marjiam's eye level. The boy, who has been half-hiding behind Jesus, comes out. Porphira gives him a big hug and

kiss. He shows no reluctance.

"Surely you're not going to take such a young disciple with You," she says.

Jesus tells her, "I was going to entrust him to one of the women."

"And not to me?" Porphira says. "I love children. I'm good with them. I help my nephews all the time."

Jesus smiles, lays His hand on her head, and says, "I brought him here because I knew you two would be a good mother and father to him." Jesus puts Marjiam's hand into theirs and says, "Bring this boy up in a holy manner. Now we will go preach by the seashore while you three get acquainted." Peter is so happy, his eyes are shining with tears. Porphira hugs Marjiam again and says, "I'm so happy! May you all be blessed."

* * * * *

In your secret place, in the presence of Jesus, examine your conscience by asking yourself:

How can I help a child who comes from a split home? How can I help this person to belong—to feel welcome and not left out?

Think about it: we have many emotional orphans in our society today, children of divorced parents, and children with working parents who have no time for them. How can you make time in your heart for them?

What would Jesus do to help them? He doesn't want anyone left out. Belonging is very important.

Song: "I Know the Father Loves Me," by Gary Ault from Beginning Today, The Dameans.

CHAPTER FORTY-SEVEN

For All

Marius is a handsome Roman soldier with a silver helmet and a fine sword. He has been watching a large crowd of Jews being healed by Jesus. The lame are walking and the blind can now see.

He is very impressed. He pushes his way through the crowd and asks Jesus, "Is this healing just for Your race, the Israelites?"

"No," replies Jesus, "My words and My healing are for all. I have come for everybody. My power is universal."

The Roman soldier stands respectfully, with his helmet off, and says, "I have an old slave who is very dear to me. He has been with me since I was a small child. He is now very sick with paralysis. I am a pagan, but I believe You are a god."

"The only slavery that disgusts me is sin," Jesus tells Marius. "But even repentant sinners receive mercy. Your slave will be cured—"

"Are you going to my house?" Marius asks.

"No, man... " Jesus smiles.

"I have asked too much. Jupiter and Apollo never go to

people's houses," the soldier says.

Jesus nods. "No, because they do not exist. But the true God enters people's houses and brings healing."

"Who is the true God?" Marius wants to know.

"He who is," Jesus replies.

"I believe You are the true God," asserts Marius.

"Yes, I am the true God. Is that not your slave?"

Marius turns around and sees an old man clad in a blanket, running....

"By Jove! It's my slave! I should say, rabbi of Israel!"

The slave replies, "I am well, Master. I felt fire going through me and I got up. I thought I heard you call. Now I can serve you."

Marius is so happy, he pulls out his purse and says to Jesus, "I should give You an offering..." then he puts his purse away and mumbles, "but this isn't enough."

Jesus replies, "Not an offering for Me, but one for the poor."

Marius says, "I'll send my slaves with a proper gift." He goes home and sends back his slaves with gold and silver. Jesus has the apostles buy food for the poor.

* * * * *

Examine your conscience by asking yourself:

Do I include everyone? Or do I leave out those who bug me?

Am I like Jesus, who was here for every race and color?

Do I put down other students because they are unpopular, or because they are poor in athletics, or poor in studies? Do I make fun of those who can't do as well as I do?

Song: "One Bread, One Body," by John Foley, SJ.

CHAPTER FORTY-EIGHT

Racism

Jesus is at Caesarea by the sea, where he sees a boy of about eight years old playing with two other small boys. Jesus calls them over and asks, "Who are you?"

"I am Lucius of Caius Marius—a Roman, the son of the Decurion of the guard."

"And who are these?" Jesus asks.

"They are Toby and Isaac; but we must be careful, or their people, the Jews, will punish them for playing with me."

"Why?'

"Because they are Jews and I am a Roman. They are forbidden to associate with us."

"But you *are* playing with them—why?"

"We like each other. We always play dice or jumping. But we have to hide or we will be beaten."

Jesus says, "Would you love Me? I am a Jew, too, and not a boy. I am a Master, something like a priest."

"What do I care?" Lucius answers, "If You love me, I will love You and I do love You, because You love me."

"How do you know I love you?" Jesus wants to know.

"Because You are good. Whoever is good loves."

Jesus turns to His apostles, who are standing nearby. "There you are, My friends—that is the secret to love. Be good, then you love without considering the person's faith or race. Remember, the Messiah came for all—not just the Jews."

The apostles stop and ponder that.

* * * * *

Ask yourself:

Do I accept all races, or do I look down on people who don't resemble me or share my beliefs or culture?

Do I remember that Jesus came for all?

Do I include all in the games we play at recess, or do I form picky groups that push others out?

Do I ask Jesus to help me be kind to any race I don't feel good about?

Song: "One Bread, One Body." by John Foley, SJ. OCP.